To Jen,
Wishing you
the very best —

Susan

The Spouse You Loved Is Gone

NOW WHAT? You're on your own, and your life feels upside-down. Yet, while you try to make sense of your loss, grief, and out-of-control emotions, you're also expected to manage the complex logistics of legal, governmental, and financial issues related to death.

Yes, *you—and only you—*are in charge of major decisions regarding wills, trusts, attorneys, taxes, budgets, Social Security, insurance ... and on and on. And while you're drowning in paperwork, you're also drowning in grief. It's an overwhelming, brutal double-whammy.

Susan Alpert has been exactly where you are. When Larry, her husband of 46 years passed away after a devastating illness, she went through all the stages of grief, depression, confusion, and just plain misery you or someone you love may be feeling right now.

In Driving Solo, Dealing with Grief and the Business of Financial Survival, she chronicles her journey from hearing that her husband has a life threatening disease, to the day he died, through hitting rock-bottom, to ultimately redefining herself and regaining control over her life.

Despite having owned and operated multimillion-dollar businesses, Susan was completely unprepared for what she now calls "The Business of Grief." What do you file first? To whom do you reach out for help? Who do you trust? Which government and financial institutions do you need to notify, and when? And how do you manage these responsibilities when you can barely get out of bed in the morning?

The book is both a love story and a tale of survival. The bonus is that in a practical, directed method Susan shows the reader how one can get through the aloneness, fear and sense of feeling completely adrift. This is the lifeline you have been looking for.

The first part of the book will help you validate your sanity, the second part, the step by step manual, will save your financial life.

Driving Solo is the first book from Susan Covell Alpert, creator of the Chaos to Control program, which coaches people through the business aspects of death and other major life changes. Alpert—a successful businesswoman, educator, and serial entrepreneur—lost her husband of forty-six years to leukemia in 2008 and found herself drowning in a sea of paperwork that only compounded her grief. Believing that no one else should have to face the confusing legal and financial obligations of loss alone, she created her step-by-step methodology, as well as her first book—a combination of the business and emotional journeys that come with the death of a spouse.

Alpert is the founder of several companies, including Motivation Resources; International Travel Incentives, Inc., which she ran for more than 35 years; The Left Handed Complement, numerous focus groups, and most recently her own consulting firm.

Alpert has a Masters of Science in Psychology and Education, and impressive experience in the fields of negotiation, finance, international services and business.

A native of Brooklyn, New York, Alpert currently splits her time between her homes in Corona del Mar and Palm Desert, California, and spends as much time as possible living life to its fullest, enjoying her daughters, their husbands and six grandchildren.

www.susanalpertconsulting.com

Driving Solo

"A compelling story of love, loss and growth. Follow Susan Alpert as she shows you how to manage the death of a loved one. Her guide is the only one you will need."

— **Dr. Steven G. Eisenberg, Renowned San Diego based oncologist**

"A beautifully written story of devotion and inner strength that captures the human soul. Larry would truly be proud of Susan's ability to turn her grief into such a positive approach to help deal with financial issues, and then to share it with all."

— **David Abrahamson, M.D.**

"It is a tough time when a spouse dies and you find yourself sifting through piles of paperwork. Susan's organized approach, simple checklist and insights into how to handle the details will help you to achieve balance – both personally, and financially."

— **C. Michael Chapman, Trust & Business Estate Attorney**

"When we lose a loved one, we have to deal with financial issues with which we're unaware. This book is the navigation you need to get your financials in order after a loss. Without guidance and direction, we will begin to wander…you must get a roadmap. Susan Alpert's book is that roadmap."

— **Wes Balakian, CEO, TrueSolutions**

Driving Solo

Dealing with Grief
and the Business of Financial Survival

SUSAN ALPERT

BARANA BOOKS

Published by Barana Books

For more information contact:
www.susanalpertconsulting.com

ISBN: 978-1-62967-019-5 (Paperback)
ISBN: 978-0-9858747-9-7 (ebook)

Library of Congress Control No: 2012951586

Printed in the United States of America

Book Design: Dotti Albertine
Cover Image: Art Wagner Photography/iStock

Dedicated to my husband
LARRY ALPERT
who made this book possible because of his life
and a necessity because of his death.

Larry, a month before receiving his diagnosis. Living life to the fullest, he had just completed 18 holes of golf, unaware that the leukemia cells had already begun their deadly work.

CONTENTS

Contents

SECTION II: THE CHAOS TO CONTROL MANUAL

And Then There Was One

And to make an end is to make a beginning.
The end is where we start from.
~T.S. Eliot, *Four Quartets*~

Once upon a time ... there was a glamorous love story; a heroine, a prince, a fairy tale wedding, and happily-ever-after. But the story doesn't end there. Our heroine moved with her prince from New York to California, raised two beautiful daughters, traveled the world, launched successful businesses, and created a community of lifelong friends – all with the man of her dreams at her side. For 46 years, it was the two of them against the world, a perfect (at least, as perfect as the real world gets) fairy tale – *until Prince Charming died.*

Then, there was just *me* – a shell of the happy heroine I had once been. It wasn't just the end of an era, or the closing of a chapter. It was, as Larry, my loving husband and the hero of the tale, put it in his final days, the end of a book – a book I had loved living. Little did I know three years ago, when it seemed as though my life was over, that it was just the beginning of another story – both the book you are holding in your hands, as well as the plotline that I am still writing for myself.

This is my story, but it could be yours. The characters, setting, and details are undoubtedly different, but in the end, we find ourselves in the same place, in the same role – the survivor, the one left to pick up the pieces and sort through the paperwork, the one who has to fight through the grief and figure out how to move forward. I cannot know exactly how you feel; I can only say that I have been there. I have lived through losing a spouse and am learning how to live again.

This book is divided into two sections. The first is a story of death and rebirth, and the insights and discoveries that helped me find my new path in life – which inspired the second part of the book, the Chaos to Control Manual. It isn't the creation of a corporate business venture or a think tank. It's the work of a grieving, educated, overwhelmed, and confused widow who didn't have a much-needed, step-by-step guide for dealing with the legal, financial, and civic aspects of losing a spouse. It was this lack of readily-available information and resources that I so desperately needed which inspired me to fill the void, so that the journey would be a bit easier for those who are just taking their first steps into life after loss.

My journey began a few years ago. Until then, I was successful, happy, and driven. My life always had purpose, as I balanced my cherished role as a loving wife and involved mother with my passion for entrepreneurship. I created successful corporations, including International Travel Incentives, which I ran for 35 years. I traveled all over the world, negotiating deals and serving high-profile clients, including Fortune 500 companies and other very recognizable names.

Then, in January 2008, my husband was diagnosed with leukemia. For the next ten months, my life was all about Larry – being his caregiver and advocate, protecting him, and spending all of my time with him. I handed off the running of my business to my employees and cleared my social calendar. My place was with him.

The world and I lost Larry in November 2008, and for the next two years, I went through the motions of being alive. My life still had some meaning – my family and friends – but my passion and purpose were long gone. I accomplished what needed to be done, traveled some, kept current with the outside world, redecorated, went out with friends, and even laughed on occasion. But what looked to others like a sad but well-functioning widow was, in reality, a lost, empty soul. Not only had I lost my loving husband; I had lost my direction in life. I had no partner, no traveling companion, and no one to take care of … or to take care of me. And I no longer had even my business to focus on. I didn't know what I wanted to do, or why, or how. And I didn't care. The future was too hard and too abstract to absorb.

Then, one evening, after a lovely dinner, my good friend Merle looked me in the eyes and asked, "What is your passion?"

I must have resembled the proverbial deer in headlights. I stared widely, hearing none of the ambient restaurant noise, seeing none of the happy diners or even the food in front of me. The realization that I had no passion overtook all my senses. In an instant, like a person facing death, my past flashed through my mind, especially the last few years. In no particular sequence, I thought about what had once been my passions. There was Larry, my business, my travels, then darkness, followed by the bright light of my daughters, their husbands, my grandchildren, and my friends. That was a temporary relief, clouded over with the reality that they all had their own lives. Regardless of their love for me, and mine for them, they had their own passions. I wasn't the center of their lives – as I had been for Larry. I had only me, without any passion to excite me or any reason to be on this earth, except to grieve.

So there I sat, knowing there was a cosmic void in me which I had no idea how to fill. I began to wonder what *would* light that fire for me, what would give me focus, direction, and purpose. I considered learning photography or bridge, neither of which I cared about at all. OK, what about joining an art appreciation group, a walking club, a current events club, or a financial management class? Nothing, absolutely nothing, interested me. Did I want to resurrect my business, be a consultant, get my Ph.D.? Once again, nothing sparked.

This continued for months. I read ads, searched the Internet for ideas, and talked to people. I was truly lost and frightened at the prospect of continuing on this path to nowhere.

Then, inexplicably, it came to me. Over the last two years of my life, in which I had been walking around in a daze, I had gained incredible experience that could actually help others. Countless people, particularly women, needed the knowledge I had gathered after Larry's death. What does one do to handle the practical aspects of settling the estate after the loss of a loved one? Whom do you notify and when? What papers do you need to file, and which documents do you need to amend? How do you untangle the pieces, and what do you do with them once there's some order? How do you tend to business when in a state of grief? I had been forced to figure all this out for myself during the darkest period of my life, when I could barely think straight, much less focus. And there had been no one-stop resource to help me sort it out. It was grueling, time-consuming, soul-ripping work. I had desperately needed someone to walk me through it all. That's what other people needed as well, I realized. They needed me.

Not only did my experiences give me the knowledge I needed to help others through this; it also gave me compassion and empathy. I understood what these people were going through because I had lived it. The Dalai Lama once said, "I believe that the purpose of life is to be happy ... and have found that the greatest degree of inner tranquility comes from the development of love and compassion." The thought of helping others made me happy; it lit me up with a fire I had not felt in some time. To do so would not only give me a purpose; it would also give some sense of meaning to my loss. Something positive would come out of the most negative period of my life. And my ever-optimistic husband would have loved that.

My mind was spinning with too many ideas. I needed a good sounding board. My dear friend Joanne sat me down and, in a very logical, business-like fashion, had me explain exactly what I wanted to relay to others. Within an hour, my plan was formulated, my message was clarified (or at least the gist of it), and I understood that my new goal was to provide grieving, overwhelmed people with the information and support they would need to move from chaos to control.

I spoke with my attorney, my accountant, and countless others whose opinions I valued. They sensibly questioned my qualifications, plans, and direction, and then told me I was on to something. I was suddenly imbued with passion that I had not felt in years. I began jotting down my thoughts on napkins, scraps of paper, legal pads, and at the computer. I wrote and wrote, often into the early hours of morning. There was so much to say.

My new venture consumed me. It was taking the place of the emptiness, but it was not just a way to fill time and distract myself, nor was it a means of self-therapy. It was greater than that. It was my purpose.

Once I had created my system (which is outlined in Section II of this book), I realized that I still had more to share. I had lived through the heartbreak of watching the love of my life battle for his, and lose. Then, with the help of an incredible grief therapist and a slew of supportive friends and family members to whom I will be forever grateful, I had fought for my own life – my life after Larry

– and chronicled that journey, from hearing that "it will get better" to actually *feeling* better. For the first time in years, I can say, with confidence, that I am alive. I laugh; I share; I feel positive and notice the goodness all around me. I am fulfilled, knowing that I can make a difference in other people's lives.

Thus, the idea for this book was born – a combination of the legal, financial, and emotional journeys that I endured on my way from the chaos of grief, back to control over my life.

While writing this book has been rewarding and even fun, it has not been easy. People have said to me, "It's so great that you're writing. That must be very cathartic." But *cathartic* implies that something makes you feel better. In reality, this book has required me to relive the most painful period of my life, and that hasn't felt good at all.

What *does* make me feel better, what has made this book worth writing, is the belief that I have something to say that other people need to hear. Although I can't take away the pain, I can at least smooth out some of the uncertainties, stumbling blocks, and detours that come with grieving for a loved one – particularly a spouse. If I only help one person, this journey will have been worth it. Perhaps that person is you.

Sue Alpert

From Grieving to Living

I know why we try to keep the dead alive:
we try to keep them alive in order to keep them with us.
I also know that if we are to live ourselves there comes a
point at which we must relinquish the dead,
let them go, keep them dead.
~JOAN DIDION, *The Year of Magical Thinking*~

Stopped in My Tracks

To be fully alive, fully human, and completely awake
is to be continually thrown out of the nest.
~PEMA CHÖDRÖN~

Larry and I were so young and naïve when we set out, hand in hand, ready to take on the world. And we did. For the next 46 years, he was my partner, best friend, and traveling companion. We visited more than one hundred countries together, and each time we took off in an airplane, we did so holding hands.

We approached the journey of life in a similar fashion – charting our course together. Our path was not always smooth or easy, and at times, it was even a bit unpleasant. Marriage, like life, has its peaks *and* valleys. But Larry and I held tightly to one another and managed to stay on course for a life that was mostly happy, and often extraordinary.

Forty-six years ago, I thought of marriage as the beginning of my adventure and approached it with the fervent passion and excitement of youth. But over time, it was the comfort, familiarity, and stability that I loved most about my relationship with Larry – the security of having a home base to which I could always return. I could be adventurous, spontaneous, and flexible at work or in my travels, because at the end of the day, Larry's safe, comforting arms would be there to stabilize and strengthen me.

In life and love, Larry grounded me, which enabled me to fly. When he died, I lost that foundation. Even the ground on which it stood crumbled beneath my feet. I could no longer fly. I was stuck, stopped in my tracks, and I was terrified.

The First Day of the Rest of His Life

Death leaves a heartache no one can heal,
love leaves a memory no one can steal.
~FROM A HEADSTONE IN IRELAND~

Months before Larry was diagnosed with leukemia, I knew something was very wrong. He had lost weight and his appetite. He was constantly chilled and tired, and had lost some of his perpetual spark. And boy, did that man sparkle! When Larry walked into a room, even when he hadn't said a word, people gravitated to him. He was tall, physically fit, good-looking, well dressed, and very funny. That was the Larry I had known since our college days. This newer version worried me.

The withdrawal was subtle. He still had that presence when he walked into a room, but when he was alone or just with family, he was more introverted than before. He still participated and made everyone laugh. He still hugged his grandchildren and told them he loved them "to the moon and back ... then on to infinity." But there was something clouded behind his eyes, and his words did not have the same intensity as before.

Suddenly, he was always cold. In early December 2007, not long before he was diagnosed, we went to visit our daughter, Bari, in San Francisco. Larry never took off his leather jacket. He just sat in a comfortable chair, bundled up. Not long after, he called on the way home from a golf tournament and complained that he couldn't get the chill out of his body, no matter how high he turned the heat in his car. He stopped and got a bowl of soup, which didn't help much, and even when he got home he could not get warm.

I saw that part of him was going. No one else could see it; they just thought he was tired. But I knew it was something else.

I shared my concerns with a few close friends, but while I was worried about his health, I never believed Larry could have cancer. Though I had been fortunate enough to know very few people with cancer, I was well-read on medical topics in general, so if I had seen someone else presenting the same symptoms, I would have undoubtedly diagnosed it. But this was Larry, so it *couldn't* be. Call it denial, but it was impossible to believe that my pillar of strength was vulnerable to something life-threatening. Larry had always been the picture of health; he ate well and exercised, sported a perpetual golf tan, and had rarely ever been sick.

Just to be sure, I had asked the doctor months before if Larry could have leukemia. My uncle had been a victim of the disease, and when I was in college, I took ill. Before we learned that it was only mono, I overheard my mother voice her fear that I might have the same deadly blood disease as her brother. So, I knew the symptoms, and Larry's low blood count and weakness raised my concern. I was petrified to say the L-word to the doctor, but I had to ask. He assured me that it wasn't likely. Larry was simply anemic. What a relief!

When the iron pills didn't help, the doctor prescribed daily B-12 shots. Surely, this would do the trick, I told myself. But as much as my mind was denying it, my soul was beginning to admit the truth: This was bad.

A few weeks later, Larry came home early from the gym. He said that something was really wrong, and that he had called his doctor's office. He was going in immediately. For Larry to admit defeat was a bad sign. Now, I was really scared. By 9:00 that morning, he was with the doctor, and several hours later we were at the hematologist's office for a bone marrow test, the first of many Larry would endure.

We were told it would take a few days to get the results, but the doctor called the next morning – January 8, 2008. Not expecting to hear from him so soon, I had already left for my appointment with the hairdresser – a decision I still regret, even though I realize my guilt is unfounded. There's no way I could have known, but I wish I had been there when Larry got the news.

When I returned home later that morning, I was startled to find Larry in "his" chair – a white, linen armchair with an ottoman, directly in front of the full-length window that framed our view of the Pacific Ocean. This was his place to read the morning paper, have conversations with me, or just enjoy the comfort and warmth of his home. But he wasn't supposed to be sitting there in the middle of a work day. Larry was an office junkie. He loved to be at work. He belonged *there* today.

I approached him with what I'm sure was concern on my face, but his expression revealed nothing. He only smiled and said my hair looked great. He waited until I had seated myself on the sofa across from him before announcing that Dr. Barke had called personally with the now present results, not wanting us to hear the bad news from a stranger. It was leukemia.

For a moment, the meaning of the word didn't register. I froze, trying to make sense of it. Then, I rushed to him. We put our arms around each other, held on tightly, and cried. After a few minutes of this, he shared the rest of what the doctor said, namely that his condition was treatable.

Larry had already sent out an e-mail with the news to his buddies. I was surprised, thinking he would be more private, but he felt comfortable telling his friends and forming a support system – one that would prove to be unbelievable over the next 10 months of chemotherapy, hospitalizations, and living away from our home and loved ones.

We immediately began our ongoing positive talks. Larry insisted that there was no question about whether he would survive, and until just weeks before he passed away, he held firmly to that conviction.

As he would write in his journal (which he was only able to do for one week, because of the chemotherapy side effects), "Apprehension and fear are slipping away, and calm confidence has been setting in. I want to beat this thing so badly. 'Who the hell do you think you are, picking on me?'" His optimism was firmly rooted in his stubbornness, and it was contagious. I believed right along with him that he would be OK, that he *had* to be OK.

I think we were both in a state of shock and ignorance. We didn't know anything about the disease – the severity, treatment, or process. Thankfully, the hematologist, Dr. Klein, agreed to meet with us a few hours later. He began the appointment by explaining that Larry had acute myeloid leukemia, or AML (incidentally, the reverse of his initials, LMA), which we later learned was the most serious and deadliest of all blood cancers. Larry would have to be hospitalized for treatment.

We naively assumed that we could take some time to plan and get things in order for Larry to be away from home for a night or two. But the doctor quickly burst that bubble, explaining that treatment would take at least a month and that he must begin immediately. Larry convinced the doctor to give him a day to take care of some things, and I had a dinner party planned for the following day. Couldn't we still have it and admit Larry on Sunday? No, Larry must be admitted to Hoag Hospital on Saturday to begin treatment.

Dr. Klein, a man we had known only minutes but who now knew more about our future than we did, explained that this disease had, at best, a 40 percent survival rate. So, *of course*, Larry would be one of the 40 percent. He wasn't a young man, but he was in better shape than most men half his age. No worries.

Besides chemotherapy, the only other course of treatment was a bone marrow transplant. He told us about Dr. Forman, a world-renowned, pioneering doctor at City of Hope Hospital who was the ultimate guru on this procedure. Dr. Klein offered to contact him about Larry, but Larry and I agreed that this would never be necessary. (How naïve we were! Later, we begged for the transplant and went through months of anxiety and disappointments until Dr. Forman, who would become the trusted man in our lives during this period, could find a match.)

We left Dr. Klein's office that day and sat in the car for quite a while, trying to make sense of what had transpired in the last few hours – how we were suddenly living such a different life than the one we woke up to. The next step was for Larry to call our two daughters, Bari and Dana. They were understandably stunned and upset, knowing that something unexpected and terrible was happening to their dad, their hero, the trunk of our family tree.

I shared the news with my brother and sister-in-law, and with two of our closest friends. That depleted all our energies; neither of us could bear to call anyone else. The only other thing I remember about that day was cancelling the dinner party while Larry called his business partner to ask if he would come over to review some papers and take the reins for the next month.

The irony of it all was that then, and for the ensuing months, we were confident that Larry would beat it and that we would continue our great life together. So, in his state of optimism (or, again, naïveté, depending on how you look at it), Larry did nothing to get our personal life in order – an oversight for which I would pay dearly in the years following his death.

We began the next morning as we often did on Saturdays. We had breakfast in the dining room, which overlooked the gardens, canyon, and Pacific Ocean. How could anything be seriously wrong? This was paradise. We played a few games of backgammon as we waited for the call from the hospital, which would mean it was time to go.

Suddenly, Larry called me over. He seemed very serious as he explained that for the first time in his life, a spiritual force, something not on this plane, spoke to him. It told him everything was going to be fine. At the time, we both interpreted this to mean that the cancer would be cured. Looking back, I think this message meant that when Larry passed to another place, everything would be OK … there. And I would be OK here. That is both my explanation and my comfort.

When the call from the hospital finally came, we collected our things and began what would be the most tremendous and deeply emotional journey of our lives.

The Relentless Pursuit of Control Amidst Chaos

Chaos is inherent in all compounded things.
Strive on with diligence.
~BUDDHA~

During the 10 months between Larry's first hospitalization and the day we lost him, I spent almost every waking minute with him. I remember telling someone that my life wasn't on hold – the hospital had actually *become* my life.

I felt capable of being in charge. I called doctor friends for advice, asked my friends to call their doctor friends, read everything I could find about leukemia, and took copious notes on the minutest details of Larry's medical care. In essence, I handled his illness like a business – something I had always been able to do successfully, something I understood, something I could control.

If I could have encapsulated Larry in a bubble, that would have been my first line of attack. The chemotherapy rendered his immune system defenseless, so he could not be exposed to any germs. The slightest infection could mean death. I began my cleaning rampage at once. There was not a surface in his hospital room that I didn't clean over and over again. The telephone, TV remote, chair frames, tables, door knobs, window sills … nothing was spared. No matter how diligent the cleaning staff was, their efforts didn't come any-where near my standards. When they left, I'd take the sanitizer and go over everything again. Any cup or straw that sat around for more than a few minutes quickly found itself in the trash. I thought I could rub away the illness, and both the room and Larry would be spotless.

No one, including me, was allowed to walk into his room with-out first scrubbing his or her hands. Whenever someone reached for the instant hand sanitizer, I cringed. *That's not good enough!* I thought. *Please, everyone, use soap and hot water, count to 100, and then dry your hands on a paper towel. Don't lean over and give Larry a hug. Don't get too close.*

For the first few weeks of chemotherapy, the body plays many cruel tricks, and Larry's wasn't spared. Still, he wouldn't admit that he was really sick. He refused to wear hospital gowns. Macho Man wasn't going to do laps around the hospital floor with some sick person's uniform flapping open in the back. So, every evening, I'd take home his pajamas and robe and, at midnight, would have the detergent and bleach swishing around the washing machine in the hottest water possible. I not only wanted to clean his clothes, I wanted to wash the leukemia away as well.

My sweet, loving, appreciative Larry finally blew the whistle. "Enough already!" he said. I could tell by his look, or perhaps I should say by his glare, that I had gone overboard. I nodded, but my stomach tightened up. I simply didn't understand how someone could be too protective when the love of her life could die from exposure to common germs.

After spending a month at City of Hope for Larry's bone marrow transplant, we were told on August 11, 2008 (our 46th wedding anniversary), that we could both move into a one-room cottage on the premises while Larry continued chemotherapy. I had been spending my nights at a nearby hotel in a questionable neighborhood so I was thrilled by the prospect of more comfortable accommodations. But more importantly, I was thrilled to be with Larry again. We hugged; we cried; we set up household like two newlyweds. I bought new pots and pans, cleaning supplies, paper plates, and permissible foods. I remember thinking it would be nice if people gave showers in these situations. I could have used a registry for all the items I bought. It was like starting all over again.

We just *knew* this would be a new beginning to a life we'd share for a long, long time. But first, of course, I had to protect and shield Larry from any foreign invasion. I removed all the bedding and pillows, bought new ones, and covered all the chairs with sheets (to be changed daily). The room was a study in antiseptic white. I cleaned, did laundry, washed windows, and cooked, hoping that Larry would be able to decipher a taste again.

The chemo destroyed his taste buds. My strapping Larry, who loved food and could usually devour huge quantities without losing his slim figure, approached each meal and snack with a gleam in his eye – as though he was thinking that maybe *this* time he would be able to distinguish salsa from ice cream. Maybe this would be the day that a pickle would have a little flavor. How disappointed he looked when there was never, and I mean *never*, a change! It broke my heart, but I kept trying.

My approach to his medications was even more protective. He took more than 30 pills every day, each with different and confusing instructions. How many red ones at this hour? Do we skip the purple one today? What strength should he have at 8:00 a.m. versus 2:00 p.m.? Is this one to be taken on an empty stomach, or with meals, or two hours before or after? I made spreadsheet after spreadsheet. I had to protect Larry from mistakes.

Then, there were the masks – the dreaded, blue surgical masks that we kept by the dozen at the door. "Larry, don't go out without a mask," I said, what felt like, a million times. "You could be exposed to a germ lurking somewhere in the trees or on a passerby. Someone could cough near you, or a carrier could sit next to you in the waiting room."

My hero, never showing that he was seriously ill, often went out to his therapy sessions merrily whistling and chatting with everyone he met. Where was the mask? He forgot. He kept forgetting, and I kept running after him. If I didn't catch him in time, I would express my disappointment upon his return. I'd accuse him of sabotaging his healing, of undoing all the precautions I was taking. I regret those words now, because in the end it wouldn't have made a difference; if anything, "forgetting" his mask only hastened the inevitable.

During a temporary remission, when Larry was well enough to go to the supermarket, I wiped down the carts. I flinched every time he touched the foods, which might have been touched by a sick person. But I bit my tongue and never verbalized those concerns.

During this period, I was probably a pain in the neck, but I didn't care. I cared about keeping Larry safe. The only protective measure that I still question (though I probably wouldn't do it any differently today) was keeping visitors at bay. I was afraid of what they might bring with them. The only exceptions were our children and grandchildren. When we were at Hoag, Dana, who lives nearby, was there every day. Steve, her husband, and our three adored grandchildren were constantly visiting – the kids scrubbing their little hands, donning their masks, and hugging and kissing their precious "Boppa." Bari and her family regularly flew down from San Francisco. She was very pregnant, but nothing would stop them. Wherever Larry was, at the hospital or during a remission at home, they were there.

The family brought light to Larry. He beamed in their presence. He relished every second with them. They had unlimited access. Everyone else was under my watchful eye, and unless they came unexpectedly (as did two of his business colleagues, who literally snuck by me to surprise him one day), I discouraged visitors altogether.

Fortunately, Larry was in concurrence with me on this one – not for the sake of his safety but because he wanted time alone with his family. As for everyone else, he was content with phone calls and e-mails. He spent hours upon hours each day communicating with the outside world, for business and mostly to keep in touch with the hundreds of friends and well-wishers who made up his support network.

I maintained control over the situation for as long as I could. All I wanted was for him to be safe and to do his part in keeping himself healthy. I don't think I believed (at least not consciously) that I could control the outcome, but I was certainly going to do everything in my power to get what I wanted. This is how I have always operated. When I set my mind to something, I work tirelessly, digging in my heels and expending all of my energy.

It took a long time for me to admit that this situation was beyond my control. And that was one of the hardest things I have ever had to do. I had put in so much effort, had tried so hard, had wanted more than anything to change things. But, in this case, nothing either of us did really mattered.

Ironically, *I* was the first to realize and accept this truth. Larry believed up until his final weeks that he was going to beat the cancer, and his certainty was so contagious that most of the time my daughters and I believed along with him. We thought we could, and would, overcome this together.

Caregiving: A Roller Coaster of Emotions

All the art of living lies in a fine mingling
of letting go and holding on.
~HENRY ELLIS~

I have proudly borne many titles in my lifetime – daughter, wife, mother, grandmother, entrepreneur, CEO, teacher, friend, and dozens of others. It was only towards the end of my living bad dream that I realized I had earned another. I was now also known as a caregiver. But that word has never resonated with me. I was Larry's wife – his advocate, best friend, and partner. When you love someone like that, you take care of each other. It's not a burden; it's just what you do, and I did it lovingly, without ever considering any other course of action. But in retrospect, I realize that this role took its toll on me – emotionally and physically.

This is true for many of the 50 million Americans – mostly women – who care for sick or elderly family members. Caregivers are 46 percent more likely than non-caregivers to report frequent mental distress and are significantly more likely to rate their health as "fair" or "poor." Caregivers also face a higher mortality rate, especially with age. For example, care-giving spouses between the ages of 66 and 96 have a 63 percent higher chance of dying than those without this responsibility.

In the scheme of things, I was very fortunate. My husband was sick for 10 months, but many people watch their loved ones waste away more slowly and suffer longer. We were able to afford the best medical professionals, who tended to most of his body's needs. Larry was a good patient – not angry or demanding. And I didn't have the financial concerns that many people face in this situation. But when I reread my journals, I am reminded that while I would have played this role for decades if necessary, and though my situation could have been worse, I wasn't exactly Pollyanna.

I was on an emotional roller coaster, with ups and downs that ran the gamut of emotions – including intense feelings of sadness, disappointment, gratitude, anger, love, under-appreciation, guilt, pain, joy, exhaustion, inundation, isolation, loyalty, protectiveness, self-pity, terror, responsibility, resentment, and too many others to list.

As the chemotherapy began to take effect, and I witnessed the side effects of the poisons ravaging the love of my life, fear became my constant companion. When the numbers on the medical charts showed a decline, I was overcome with anguish. Conversely, given any trace of hope, I became elated. This continued until the very end. I never felt stable or grounded – only constant anxiety about what emotion would come next.

After a few weeks of caregiving, exhaustion took over. I was doing so much. I was the laundress, the food deliverer, the sanitizer, the communicator, the lover, the parent, the company president, the go-fer, the bill payer, the household administrator, the cheerleader, the researcher ... ad infinitum. Between my overwhelming responsibilities and my overpowering emotions, I could hardly catch my breath – much less process my complicated emotional state.

To make matters worse, I have fibromyalgia, a neurological disorder that causes chronic pain and fatigue, which only exacerbated my emotions. Still, I was at Larry's bedside every day, from early in the morning until 9:00 p.m. or later. I did my best to put on an effervescent act, to never let him see that I was tired or frightened, or in pain. My job (and it was so very hard) was to keep him worry-free and comfortable. After all, *he* was the cancer patient. It was all about Larry. Anyone who has ever been a caregiver knows exactly what I mean.

Although I felt tired and overwhelmed, I was never bitter. It didn't feel like a sacrifice, or something about which I had a choice.

This was the only thing to do, because along with all the negative emotions that plagued me during this time, I was also overcome by the love I felt for my "patient." There was joy in holding his hand, in giving him all I could and more, in going out of my way to please him and help him in his recovery, in knowing that I was doing everything I possibly could to make this ordeal more tolerable for him. When he smiled and joked, my heart swelled with happiness and the satisfaction of a job well done.

The cold, hard fact was that I was riddled with guilt that I couldn't do more, that I hadn't acted earlier, that I occasionally lost patience with Larry, and that I got angry with him and showed it. But at times, I felt underappreciated. Though Larry always thanked me for coming to be with him and for everything I did, I secretly wanted more (though I had no idea what "more" was). And that line of thinking always brought me back to guilt. How selfish could I be? This man was in excruciating pain, and probably afraid, although he never once showed it. Who was I to want more from him? I felt that I was a bad person. It never occurred to me that I was only human … and an exhausted, terrified, stressed one at that.

It is only in retrospect that I clearly see how difficult and exhausting life was for me during this time. But I quickly learned that my complicated emotional state was something I shared with all caregivers. I met others in the hospital who were just as anxious and upset. Knowing I was not the first person to have these experiences, nor would I be the last, made me feel less isolated, and less guilty about my "selfishness." Soon, I had become part of a community of caregivers. We came from all different walks of life, but we had at least one thing in common. We all ended up needing our own caregivers.

For me, however, there was an additional emotional element to my new role as caregiver. We've all heard stories about women who look in the mirror one day only to realize, with surprise, that the face of their mother is staring back at them. I had a similar experience while caring for Larry, and my feelings were more than a little conflicted over the sudden awareness.

Growing up in 1940's Brooklyn, my childhood was much like that of my neighborhood friends. Yes, I took care of my elderly grandmother, and yes, I knew that my mother's brothers had far more money than we did, but in general I thought our family looked just like any other. We were happy, there was unconditional love, laughter, and we were always surrounded by a large network of family and extended family.

In truth, I later learned, my mother was perpetually dissatisfied with her life. Intelligent, witty, accomplished, and strong, she was nonetheless denied the opportunity of furthering her education as her brothers had. As a woman living in the early 1900s, she was expected to take typing and care for her family. In an awful twist of fate, she eventually typed all of her brothers' college papers and medical school documents, acquiring, secondhand, the formal knowledge that was denied to her. As I grew older, my mother was adamant that I do well in school and avoid any classes that focused on typing or shorthand. According to her, there were better things in store for me – a bachelor's and master's degree, as it turned out.

Then, after years of raising her family, my mother was also forced to take on the role of caregiver to my father, after he suffered a serious stroke that left him unable to do much beyond the basics. Suddenly, my mother wasn't just tending to her children but also to a husband who could no longer care for himself. The strain, added to an already difficult life, took its toll on my mother's health.

My mother never lived to see my successes, but I know she would have been proud of the career and life I built. Throughout the early days of my marriage and family, I often thought of her, especially when Larry and I took our children to Hawaii for a family vacation – a trip that would have been impossible for my constantly struggling mother.

However, in August of 2008, I finally started to realize the true extent of my mother's struggles as I found myself in increasingly similar circumstances, reliving aspects of her existence that had made her so very unhappy and even ill.

Living in the one-room bungalow with Larry as he underwent his treatment, I watched my husband waste away, much as my father had. In addition, my responsibilities changed from running a business to household chores – cleaning, washing, and cooking (a task I had always hated). Many days I found myself, broom in hand, sweeping the front patio and chatting with our neighbors, exactly as my mother had done for decades while I was growing up. I would also meet the other ladies at the washing machines—outdated devices that had probably been around even when my mother was doing laundry. Everything about my life was starting to look familiar … uncomfortably familiar.

For me, it was a chance to finally understand what my mother had gone through. More than ever I wished I could talk to her, adult to adult. I would give her the biggest hug and thank her from the depths of my soul for everything she taught me, giving me the strength to stand up straight and carry on, just as she had. Now, when I look in the mirror, I hope I see her, I hope I feel her strength and courage, and pray that it passes on to me. Unlike some women, I would be proud to look in the mirror and find that my face and my mother's face had intertwined.

So despite my sudden acquaintance with a variety of caregivers at the hospital, my mother was actually my first template for all of the difficult times I would experience throughout Larry's cancer, especially in regards to my health.

Caregivers – and grievers – do not take care of themselves. And we pay the price for this neglect. While I was frustrated with Larry for refusing to acknowledge the limitations of his body, I did a good job of ignoring mine as well. During those 10 months, I never analyzed my emotions. Who had time? Larry was *dying*. My suffering wasn't important, so I worked hard to hide it. But I couldn't always hide the toll it took on my health.

I tried to take care of myself. I ate regularly, albeit hospital cafeteria fare was the norm, and brought exercise clothes with me to the hospital so I could slip out for a walk. I took my vitamins, slept as much as possible at night (with the help of my favorite prescription sleep aids), and even napped when I could. I had outside contact with the world and did routine maintenance for myself. But all of these perfunctory efforts didn't make up for the damage the emotional turmoil was doing to my body.

I was beyond exhaustion. My body parts took turns screaming for attention. Too often they worked in pairs or groups, or clustered together as one big whole. But I ignored the warning signs my body was trying to give me and pushed through it.

During Larry's battle with cancer as well as in the years following his death, I had two hospital stays, spent six weeks housebound, visited the emergency room, and had ongoing doctors' appointments and tests. Along with the fibromyalgia, I suddenly and unexpectedly suffered a rare form of colitis, developed recurring pneumonia in both lungs, and endured a series of serious and not-so-serious medical conditions. I was too stubborn to care for myself and too independent to let others help. And I paid for my foolishness. (This is why there is an entire section in the Chaos to Control Manual on "Taking Care of Yourself.")

Larry and I endured cancer together, both in our own ways. Larry knew this as well as I did, and he spoke of it as "our" illness.

But while I eventually recovered my health, he was not so lucky.

In those last few weeks, Larry *really* suffered. At first, I begged him to hold on. I pleaded with the Universe to let me keep him, to just give me a little more time. But I watched his condition continue to worsen – the dramatic weight loss, the labored breathing, the moaning and occasional cries of pain, the fog that settled into his eyes, the inability to communicate or eat, the tubes and machines, the utter devastation of the strong body that held me for most of my life. The more he suffered, the more clear it became to me that I would have to let go, and the more I wanted him to stop fighting.

My daughters and religious leader were not ready to give up and tell him that his time on Earth had ended. They told me to have hope – and not to deflate or take away his confidence. But all of the "ologist" specialists and I knew they were wrong. I struggled for an answer, but in my heart I knew I had to let Larry know. He was responsible for himself in his lifetime; he had every right to know this part as well. I finally told Larry that we'd reached the end of the line, and that it was OK to go. I promised him that the girls and I would take care of each other, and that while we'd always miss him, we would go on with our lives to honor the family he and I created.

In the end, I stopped begging Larry to hold on and started pleading with him to let go. The last week was so horrible for him that my desire to have him here began to matter far less than my desire to see him at peace. In those moments, nothing was more important than stopping his pain – even though that meant pain and loneliness for me. But I could handle my pain; watching his was unbearable.

We stayed at the hospital in Hoag, where Larry was sent back for his final round of chemotherapy, until about 36 hours before he died. The doctors were clear that nothing else could be done; we were on the home stretch. I asked Larry if he wanted to stay or go home. Understanding that he was choosing where he would die, he very softly and weakly spoke two words: "Go home." These were the only two words he had spoken in more than a week.

At Hoag Hospital, Larry was cared for by numerous warm, compassionate attendants. I asked one of them, a nurse named Mo, if he would take some vacation time and come home with us to help care for Larry in his final hours. It wasn't a hard sell. Larry was very well-liked by all the staff. That night, the doctor came in to speak with us and left with his head in his hands.

The next morning, Mo and I took Larry home. My son-in-law, Steve, who dearly loved Larry, had removed the furniture from our living room to clear the way for a hospital bed, from which Larry could see the home we built together one last time. In truth, I don't know if Larry ever knew he was home. By the time we got there, his mind seemed to be gone. Dana said that he smiled at her once, and she believes he knew where he was, but I'm not convinced.

I spent that day and night at Larry's side – holding his hands, caressing his body, kissing his forehead, and whispering words of love and comfort. I have read that hearing is the final sense a dying person loses, so although Larry could not respond to me, I gently spoke to him.

I took a few short breaks. During one of them, while I was resting around midnight, Mo came to tell me that it was time. I went in to be with Larry, to tell him again how much I loved him and that his family would be OK.

Within minutes, the life left the man who had, to me, always seemed so much larger than life. When he took his final breath, it was just the two of us – just as when we first started out.

When he was gone, I was hit with a whirlwind of emotions – shock, disbelief, relief that he was no longer suffering, and great sadness. I did not become hysterical. In that moment, I didn't even cry. I would do plenty of that later, but for now, I was just numb.

I stepped back to call the girls and let the nurses and funeral directors do their job. Larry was gone; there was only a body left. I no longer felt the need to control anything.

This was the end of the journey for Larry and, I thought, for me as well.

Driving Solo

Sometimes, when one person is missing,
the whole world seems depopulated.
~LAMARTINE~

Suppose you've been driving down the same road for a long time. It's familiar and predictable. You know what to expect and how to handle its twists and turns, so navigating it requires very little concentration.

Suddenly, the familiar road disappears. Perhaps you had advance warning; perhaps you did not. Either way, it's simply not there one day. You can't turn around. You can't bring back what was. You panic. You know that if you try to continue forward, you'll harm yourself and others, or get stuck somewhere. You might even drive into nowhere.

Now, what if you'd always been the passenger, shared the responsibility, or relied on your GPS? You never really paid much attention to how you were getting to your destination because you never had to. But now you're alone, *and* the road has changed. You're confused, frightened, and overwhelmed. What do you do?

Imagine this scenario if you're also in grief, if you've recently suffered such a significant loss that you're in constant pain, feeling alone and abandoned. How are you supposed to work yourself out of the mire and find a new course if you can barely think straight?

This is how I felt during the first couple years following Larry's death – when I was suddenly driving solo on a road I didn't recognize, *without* my co-pilot and the security that he had always offered, and with grief, fear, and panic as my only companions. To make matters worse, none of my friends had yet traveled this path, so they couldn't offer any guidance.

I felt alone (just me, myself, and I) as I was thrown through one loop after another – the paperwork, the finances, simple trips to the grocery store, trying to put on a happy face. Even getting out of bed in the morning felt like a U-turn. I just wanted to crawl back under the covers and hide. How was I supposed to do it all alone?

But, like it or not, I was in the driver's seat now. And since stopping the car and getting out would mean losing everything Larry and I had worked to build, I had no choice but to keep driving. The trick, I learned, is that while I was the one behind the wheel, I didn't have to be the only one in the car. It took some time for me to emerge from the cocoon of isolation and self-misery I had built for myself, but when I finally started asking for help, I found the courage to drive on.

The Journey Back to Happiness

When you are sorrowful look again in your heart,
and you shall see that in truth you are weeping
for that which has been your delight.
~KHALIL GIBRAN~

"He's in a better place now." "Everything happens for a reason." "This, too, shall pass." People use a lot of clichés when attempting to comfort the bereaved. In all fairness, they do this because they don't know what else to say and they truly want to help. But in reality, clichés are only words, and they provide little relief to a woman grieving the loss of her husband. In fact, after hearing, "You will not feel like this forever" (or some variation of that) for the umpteenth time, I wanted to scream at my well-meaning friends and family members, "That isn't doing me any good right *now*, is it?"

A few months after Larry passed away, I sat on the sofa in my grief therapist's office, tightly clutching a well-used box of tissues, rubbing my eyes, and vainly asking for reassurance. "Marilyn, when will this all be over?" I asked. "This ache, this despair, this state of depression."

With deep compassion and a clear knowing, she softly and frankly told me what she had learned from many years of working with the bereaved: It would take about three years for me to feel "normal" again. Well, not *normal*, she said. Normal implies that things would be the same, and to tell someone who's recently lost a spouse that life will ever be the same is simply off base. But I would feel good, happy, and content, she said. I would feel like myself again, though perhaps a different version of myself.

"Until then, you will face the most intense pain a human can endure," she explained. "You will be caught in a chronic yo-yo pattern."

The first year, she said, would be a blur of constant pain, paperwork, creating useless diversions, and aimlessly moving an object from one room to another, then mindlessly moving it back or someplace else. "The first year is about the person you lost," she concluded. "The second year, it becomes about you."

Perhaps she talked about positive aspects of the first year, but all I remember thinking is, *I'll never make it through this year, much less the rest of my life.* Forcing myself to keep it together, I reasoned that at least I would be fine by the second year. I could look forward to that.

Nope. The second year would be rough as well, according to Marilyn. It would be the time in which I would have to rediscover who I was, separate from Larry. I'd have to reacquaint myself with the "real me."

I didn't understand what that meant but I knew I didn't like it. It was a scary thought. I didn't want to know anything else about me. I just wanted to be happy and pain-free. What I really wanted was my old world back again. I glanced at the door, wishing there was a clock on the wall to tell me that this session was over, that I could run out and pretend that what she said wasn't true. But it proved to be so, so true.

When she added that relief would come somewhere in the third year, I quickly did the math. That meant I would be whole and functioning again sometime in 2012! I shuddered at the idea. Getting through the rest of this session felt impossible. Three more years? At the time, I was certain that she was wrong. She *had* to be wrong.

As I write this book, it is three years later, and I can attest that Marilyn was right on target. During the first year, I cried all the time, but in my state of raw grief and exhaustion, I didn't think much about the future, just about getting through the day. In year two, I was confronted with the realization that I no longer had a path or a purpose in life. And I had to answer the most primal and important question of all, a question I thought I had already answered: Who am I? I had been part of "Larry and Sue" for two-thirds of my life. I had no idea how to be just "Sue."

Those first two years were a wild ride which plunged me to the depths of myself, taking me through twists and turns of grief, isolation, and reflection, and finally dropping me off in a place of peace. About halfway through the third year, I CAME BACK!

I regained my health and strength. I discovered the power of women's friendships and am grateful to have been surrounded by an amazing number of loving people, whom I cherish dearly. I rediscovered simply being alive, and I now appreciate each and every moment to be with others or myself. After years of misery, I savor the world again. I am living.

These may sound like the words of a cancer survivor – someone who approached the brink of death but was given a reprieve. In reality, I was the caregiver to a cancer patient. I shared every second of Larry's illness, but unlike him, I was given a second chance. He fulfilled his purpose in this life. And while grieving for him, often wishing I could join him in death, I found my own reason to get out of bed in the morning, one surprisingly independent of Larry, but certainly inspired by him.

But first, I had to find the courage to experience the most hopeless, frustrating, painful days of my life. And I had to do the impossible: Learn to live without Larry.

The Pretend Life Didn't Work for Me

Sorrow makes us all children again – destroys all
differences of intellect. The wisest know nothing.
~Ralph Waldo Emerson~

I remember once hearing that if we act as if something is true, it will become true. Following Larry's death, I sometimes acted as if my life was continuing, as if it had any semblance of normality left. I mandatorily went to the dentist and the hairdresser, met with the accountant, and occasionally had lunch or dinner with a friend. I even ventured into the supermarket. Who was I kidding? I'm sure I babbled on and on, and then listened without hearing, focused on the noise inside my head rather than those around me.

There were times when I really pulled it off, though – when everyone in the room (but me) thought that I was healing. I have actually had some practice at pretending, thanks to my fibromyalgia. People with chronic pain disorders like mine, or any medical issue that other people can't see, often learn to act as though they feel fine, even when they are so uncomfortable that it is hard to concentrate or enjoy what's going on around them.

Larry, however, could always tell when I didn't feel well. I know from talking to others with pain syndromes that there are often one or two people in our lives who know us so well that they can see through our most Oscar-worthy performances. Larry and I had a running joke about my "clone" or "sister." At the end of a night out, he would come into our bedroom and find me curled up, looking miserable, sometimes even softly crying, and say, "How can you pull yourself together and look and act so happy and bubbly when you're not feeling well? We step out of the house, and it's another you – that clone, that sister who comes out of the closet and really pulls it off." He would frequently joke, "What did you do with my wife? Where are you hiding her?"

After attending my first social event following what I refer to as DD ("Death Date"), I penned a letter to Larry in my journal (something I did often), in which I wrote: *"Went to a wedding tonight – pulled it off OK. You would have been proud of my social and physical sister – my clone."* And I did pull it off, outwardly. Inwardly … that was another story.

At the wedding, I was dressed in evening attire, sporting four-inch heels and perfect makeup. I was outgoing and social, acting "as if" so well that I almost fooled myself … until I went into the restroom. When I was alone, I suddenly didn't want to go back out. But I put on more blush, applied another layer of unneeded lip gloss, and made myself walk back into the reception. Then, I automatically did what I always did whenever I came out of a restroom or walked away from a table where I had been mingling. I looked around for the tallest, most handsome guy in the room, expecting to find Larry, to whom I would go and be safe and secure. But of course, the tallest guy in the room wasn't Larry. Now, where was I supposed to go? To whom did I gravitate?

When they played our song – "Fly Me to the Moon" – I *really* went into my head. That was another bitter taste of being without Larry where it made a difference, and it was heart-wrenching.

For the most part, I did a pretty good job convincing people – especially those to whom I was not particularly close – that I wasn't on the verge of a nervous breakdown, that I was the same strong, put-together, even stoic person I had always been. But there were other times when the reality of my grief made me act like a different person, a stranger even to myself.

I vividly recall a trip to the local gourmet market shortly after DD. I placed one apple, one orange, two bananas, and a small container of soy milk in the cart. When I gazed down at my selection, the lonely, empty, wire basket shouted out to me, "You're alone! You're pathetic! Larry's really gone." There was no reason to shop, to live, to act "as if" anymore.

Suddenly, I was interrupted by one of my neighbors, who wanted to offer her condolences. Her nervousness was reflected in her hug; the uncertainty about what to say showed in her face. What did she know about how I felt? Her cart was brimming with shiny, healthy, colorful vegetables – probably for a salad to accompany the meats, rolls, and other goodies she was buying to feed her family. When she got home, someone would greet her, give her the customary peck on the cheek, and ask, "How was your day, sweetheart?" All this would no doubt play out as a ho-hum, everyday routine, one without much thought or gratitude for the moment. But what *I* wouldn't have done for such an inconsequential, unexciting moment with my husband! I was returning alone to my silent home, which would never again be filled with Larry's playfulness or laughter, or even our disagreements, which I would have welcomed with open arms.

My reaction to all this was simple – and completely out of character. Right there, in the middle of the bread aisle, I began to sob noisily, put on my dark sunglasses, abandoned the cart with its meager contents, and fled – trying to look dignified despite my hunched shoulders and wet cheeks. I didn't venture into another market for more than a month. Thankfully, I discovered that you can order anything (even food) online and I lived that way for a while. When in need, Google had an answer. I still ordered my one apple and one chicken breast, and everything else I needed, but I was able to get them while shielding myself from reality.

I have shed few tears in my life, not because they weren't warranted, but because I learned very early in life to build a thick, protective barrier around my heart. You see, I became well acquainted with death as a child. Before age 24, I'd lost both parents, as well as grandparents, aunts, uncles, friends, and other loved ones. I made a list of all the deaths I can remember before I even had children of my own, and came up with 23.

Losing Larry, however, was an entirely different story. And to make matters worse, I was suddenly grieving not only for him, but for all the other loved ones who died before him, whose deaths I didn't fully absorb because I had Larry to comfort me, because I could always tell myself that I would never be truly alone as long as I had him. The pain was excruciating, paralyzing, and overwhelming.

In the first year after DD, the breakdowns – public and private – happened more frequently than I would have liked.

Several weeks after the grocery store incident, on a sunny Friday afternoon, I was brought to my knees over a water leak. There were people in the house with me – my friend Joanne, my daughter, the housekeeper, and some workmen, who were there to find out why my bedroom carpet felt damp. When they told me I had a slab leak and that repairing it would involve tearing up the flooring and breaking into the interior and exterior walls, which would disrupt my life for weeks, I – who was always in control and tended to take mundane matters like home repairs lightly – reacted completely out of character. I lost all control. I ran outside, crouched against the wall, and once again sobbed desperately, as though there was someone else in my body.

I didn't feel, as I have heard people describe, that I was on the outside of my body looking in. Rather, I was on inside looking out, but the insides were different than before. I had never understood the depths of a broken heart. Now, I was broken inside and couldn't pull it all back together. I had no strength with which to help my protective wall stand. It just melted and left me with raw insides.

This couldn't be me. Sue Alpert would never be brought to her knees by a slab leak. How tragic I had become! I was frightening myself and my loved ones. I remember the looks on their faces, especially my gentle housekeeper, who came outside with a box of tissues and a glass of water and awkwardly tried to comfort me. The sympathy, love, and worry on her face brought me back to reality. I couldn't do this to those who cared about me. I told myself, "Pull yourself together and act as if." And I did.

When everyone left, I gave myself permission to be afraid, to feel out of control, to worry about me, and of course, to cry myself to sleep in what was once our bed, but now just mine. This is how I coped for the next year, with maybe one or two more public breakdowns along the way.

Eventually, after much soul searching, a way out presented itself – a calling, a purpose, a new direction. I didn't have to pretend anymore. Yes, my life would continue but it would never be the same. I would have to redefine "normal" … and I was going to need some help.

Seek Help ... and Ye Shall Find It

While grief is fresh, every attempt to divert only
irritates. You must wait till it be digested, and then
amusement will dissipate the remains of it.
~SAMUEL JOHNSON~

We all grieve in own ways, on our own schedules. And we all find means for recovery that are unique to our situations, personalities, and temperaments. For some, support groups are the answer. Others prefer individual therapy. Some talk to clergy, friends, and family in lieu of professional help, and others manage on their own. After a few weeks on my own, and a few hours in a support group, I found the right course for me.

It was three weeks after Larry's funeral, and I was still walking around in a state of shock and disbelief. People around me seemed to just go about their daily routines; they laughed, got angry, went to work, and ate dinner. Didn't they know that there was no longer a world? Why weren't their eyes glossed over with lids that kept wanting to close and shut out the world? What mattered anymore? Nothing.

I was told over and over by well-meaning loved ones to go to a support group, to spend some time with people who could truly understand what I was going through. But I didn't want to leave the house or talk to anyone. Then, one day, as I absentmindedly thumbed through the morning paper, a notice jumped out at me. It was for a cancer survivors' support group at Hoag Hospital – familiar territory for me – and it met that night at 5:30 p.m., the perfect time. Other people would be preparing for their family dinners, but I had no one to prepare for.

Reacting, rather than analyzing, I went. I almost turned around when I reached the parking lot. I felt confused and unsure. Where was I going? Was this the right building? Was it the right time? I didn't trust myself. Once inside the building, I couldn't find the room. I felt like I was in a maze with the walls closing in on me. My throat was dry. I forced myself into auto-pilot and walked through the doors.

Sitting around a long table were about a dozen people, many older, some well-groomed, some in business attire, others rumpled and weary. Where did I belong? I was dressed, made up, put together. I felt like they were all watching me, trying to figure out why I was here, while I wondered the same thing about them.

Then, in walked this young, beautiful woman with alabaster skin, black hair, beautiful eyes, and a smile that would put anyone at ease. She took her place at the head of the table. *Wow*, I thought, *this is* some *therapist*. That turned out to be the understatement of the century. This woman, Marilyn Kaplan, was to become my lifeline, the person who took me from the depths of sorrow to heights I thought I'd never see again.

Marilyn asked us to introduce ourselves, and then to name the person who had died, the cause, and the full date. I hate this type of banter but had no choice except to participate. When it was my turn, I confidently said my name was Susan and that Larry, my husband of 46 years, had died of leukemia a few weeks earlier. Marilyn asked me to state the full date, and I softly, with less confidence, replied that I didn't know. That was my first wake-up call. I was living in such a thick fog that I could not remember the date my life as I knew it ended. Clearly, I had a lot of work ahead of me and little understanding about what that would entail.

I sat through the session, listening to the other people tell their tragic stories and occasionally share an upbeat moment from the past week. I felt so out of place. I was truly sorry for their losses, for the tears running down their faces, for their sobs and nose blowing, for their despair. But it wasn't mine. I lost *Larry*. Couldn't anyone understand that?

A sophisticated woman, battling not only the death of her husband, but also alienation and legal disputes with his family, leaned forward and spoke proudly. It had been six months since her husband's death, and over the weekend, she had cleaned out his closet and given away all his clothes. That was her great achievement for the week? My stomach knotted up. I could never do that.

Of course, I did do it – many months later. And while I knew it had to be done, it did not feel like an achievement. It felt like a betrayal, as if I was erasing all of him, as if he would come home to find his belongings and treasures gone and be so disappointed and angry with me.

One middle-aged gentleman, whose wife had been a painter, announced that he was getting ready to give away her works. Everyone was disposing of the remains, like the corpses they buried. My mind screamed, *Get me out of here! This is not for me!* I tolerated the remainder of the meeting, hearing nothing but garbled sounds coming from the couple holding hands and leaning on each other as they talked about the loss of their adult son.

The ray of light was Marilyn, whose wisdom, kindness, and insight captivated me. I returned to the group only one more time before deciding that I couldn't take any more. My grief was still too intense for me to find relief in someone else's pain and story. When this insufferable experience was over, however, I approached Marilyn and asked if she offered individual therapy. She gave me her card, and I called for an appointment the next day – the first, but crucial step on my long, arduous journey to peace and wholeness.

Grief 101

Grief is itself a medicine.
~William Cowper~

From Marilyn, I learned about how to survive in an unfamiliar world I had never fully visited, a place she called *Grief World*. I interpreted this to mean a state in which a mourner exists that has no resemblance to any other place they've known. In fact, unless you reside there in your lifetime, you'll never understand. But if you've been unfortunate enough to be part of this non-exclusive club, you'll know what I mean. In *Grief World*, your thought process is confused, your memory weak, your actions erratic, your body unresponsive, and your capabilities diminished. Your thresholds are lowered, and your emotions go from non-existent to exaggerated, sometimes in a split second. I lived there for years.

Marilyn introduced me to another of her coined-phrases – the *tear storms* that would be part of my life for a long while, the racking, uncontrollable crying that has a life of its own. I understood what she meant. These storms, which came with torrential force, would last for hours and then let up, only to reappear for no particular reason. Marilyn reiterated that this would continue, but with grief work, the frequency and power of the *tear storms* would lessen. Could I believe it at the time? Not at all. Did the pain suddenly disappear? Not at all. But with time, much time, and with practice, much practice, her wisdom brought results.

After several sessions, Marilyn began to give me concrete assignments to complete at home between sessions. As much as I was grasping for hope and survival, some of these tasks seemed beyond my capability – too much, too soon, or at least I thought. But she said they were "non-negotiable," because the only way to get through my grieving process was to really feel the pain. If I didn't start feeling my feelings, my healing would take significantly longer. There was even a chance I'd never get past my grief and become a lifetime mourner. I was both relieved to have someone to guide me and scared by the prospect of having to take action. But I didn't know how I was going to live like this for the next few months, much less a lifetime. So, I became a model student and did what I was told.

The first step was to do something about my diet. I've never known anyone in *Grief World* who ate healthy, balanced, regularly-scheduled meals. When Marilyn asked about the contents of my pantry, she learned that, other than the days when my daughter or friends deposited home-cooked meals on my kitchen counter, I was living on a steady diet of peanut butter from the jar, dry cereals, and frozen chocolate yogurt. This was not from a lack of appetite. If anything, I have always tended to comfort-eat. But these "meals" didn't require preparation, and I'd never been one to spend much time in the kitchen. I proved early on in our marriage that I was a good cook, but it was never a task I enjoyed. So, Larry and I ate most of our meals out. Of course, without Larry, I didn't much feel like going out.

Marilyn's direction – which felt more like a commandment – was to focus on the basic needs of survival. I was to go to the market and buy at least six frozen dinners, completely disregarding the labels screaming about salt, trans fats, sugar, calories, and unpronounceable chemicals. The goal was to get food back into my system. Later on, we added foods that actually came from the ground.

Another non-negotiable was to get dressed six out of seven mornings each week. There were many days when just getting out of bed and working in my office felt like a crushing weight on my body. My snuggly robe and fuzzy slippers seemed like the perfect wardrobe. But Marilyn instructed me to shower the moment I got up and then to dress in real clothing.

While this assignment was not one I particularly *wanted* to do, I understood the reasoning. When my children were little, if I wanted them to go a certain place and act a certain way, I would have them dress up. The minute they put on pretty dresses, they acted differently. It's similar to when a woman has a good hair day. Suddenly, she is more confident. Her posture is better. She stands taller and holds her chest higher, and *hopes* she runs into someone she knows.

In my bathrobe, I felt like I should be back in bed like it was OK to just pull the covers over my head and hide from the world. It was easier to do nothing. In real clothes, I felt more put together, less of a victim. I wasn't as tragic. Because I was dressed like a person, I had to act like a person.

Next, Marilyn ordered me to get out of the office in which I had imprisoned myself with the task of settling our finances and business affairs (more on this in Section II). Though I am generally a very social being, during the first year and a half after DD, I refused invitations to be with friends and family. It was simply too difficult to explain what I was going through, and none of my friends had lost their spouses.

I also knew that I was a downer to be around. I had nothing to contribute to conversations other than my repetitive woes. I was overwhelmed with paperwork and spent every day in my office, jumping back and forth between the computer and the piles of paper that needed my attention. I was extremely critical and hard on myself. I wanted to perform perfectly and didn't feel as though I was progressing quickly enough. Besides, if I kept frantically busy, there would be no time to feel the emotional pain and despair.

Marilyn insisted that I cross "to-dos" off my calendar one day a week. I wasn't allowed to check e-mail. I was to shut down the computer, lock up my office, and escape. For a workaholic, this was one of her hardest non-negotiables. I equated it with quitting smoking, giving up chocolate, or overcoming any other addiction. The compulsion to jump back in was so powerful, but the need to heal was just a little greater, so I followed her instructions. I admit that I did this kicking and screaming, rebelling like a cornered child, but it was exactly what I desperately needed. I wasn't in an emotional place where I could sit still, meditate, or read a book. But I did begin to create a little balance in my life. Leaving my office may seem like a baby step, but for me, it was a giant leap.

In time, when Marilyn felt I was ready, we moved on to even bigger steps. First, I removed all pictures of Larry from our bedroom. Later, I cleaned out Larry's closet and donated his clothes to charity. I even redecorated. Marilyn insisted that it was important for me to make the space mine, so that everything in the house didn't remind me of Larry, so that I could begin to see my home as the comfortable place where I live, not the sad place where Larry *used* to live. With help from my close friend and interior designer, Myra, I transformed our bedroom loft into a soft, beautiful retreat with ceiling-to-floor windows that provided an endless view of the sailboats along the Pacific, and pieces of art that Larry never saw. I even began sleeping on "his" side of the bed. I now had something that was mine alone, not ours. It was painful, but the room was so lovely, and I was grateful for the calming space.

I could devote chapters and chapters to the ways in which Marilyn helped me get comfortable with (and then get out of) *Grief World*. But I'll conclude with the most powerful, most controversial, and most difficult assignment of all. This one I fought, avoided in the beginning, questioned its worth versus its potential damage, constantly complained about, and absolutely dreaded. Even today, thinking of it brings back painful memories, but I cherish the results.

Marilyn suggested that I make what she called a *grief box*. In this treasure trove, I was to place a few items that were special to Larry or that I felt truly represented him. I included his signature watch, his driver's license, the family pictures he carried with him, a bracelet I bought for him that he never took off, some foreign coins that held special memories, and even a Chinese fortune-cookie message that was especially meaningful to us.

Then, I was to light a candle and devote an hour (yes, a complete hour, 60 minutes, 3,600 seconds) each day, at the same time, to sitting alone with the contents of the box, without music or any other distractions. It sounds like torture, I know, and it certainly was. I would spread the items out in front of me and fondle them, evoking idealized memories of days long past while I sobbed and sobbed. I never lasted an hour and occasionally skipped days. During the time with my *grief box*, I felt that my body and soul had been taken over by a cruel, unknown force. Then suddenly, with no explanation, the *tear storms* would stop (if only for a little while), and I would be released from the intense pain.

I shared this process with my best friend, Myrna, and my daughters, who questioned what I was doing. They believed I should be thinking happy, positive thoughts, not dwelling in a place of darkness where I constantly replayed my story of losing Larry. They suggested I try another therapist and experience his or her methods. I understood and appreciated their concern, but that little voice inside of me reassured me that I was on the right path, with the perfect guide. My vulnerability to follow Marilyn's instructions was more than weakness and fear of starting something new; it was a need to finally give up control and let someone else drive, someone whom I knew

I could trust for reasons I couldn't then put into words. But my gut intuition told me this was the way out.

Marilyn understood something about me that my friends and family didn't. And neither did I, at least, not yet. I *needed* to feel the pain. I had spent a lifetime putting up walls so I could avoid dealing with unpleasant emotions. Now that Larry was gone, so was my wall. And those emotions I had suppressed for decades were now suppressing my ability to get out of bed in the morning. The only way to get them under control was to give up control, and to let myself *feel* – even though it hurt like nothing I'd ever imagined.

Anxiety and terror accompanied me each time I sat down with my *grief box*. My belief that this, like the *tear storms*, would eventually decrease in frequency and intensity kept me going. And, in time, it worked. One night, months later, as I prepared to go to bed (something I dreaded), I reflected on my day and realized that I hadn't cried for hours. What was happening? Was it a false alarm of hope, or just a flashing glimpse that change was possible? Once again, the unknown frightened me.

I faced that initial period of grief head on – not pushing the pain back down again so that it could re-emerge years later or even hold me back from moving forward with a full life. Though there were days during this period when I might not have believed it, I *wanted* to live. I wanted to be happy again. I just needed to learn how.

STAGE 3

Endings and Beginnings

Whichever road I take, the guiding star is within me, the
guiding star and the loadstone which points the way. They
point in but one direction. They point to me.
~Ayn Rand~

I spent years mired down in the quicksand that Marilyn called
Grief World, where I was going through the motions of being alive
but not really going anywhere at all. Then, just when I thought I
might as well unpack and settle down, I began to see the way out
– the way back to all the people who were missing me in the real
world, back to freedom and joy, back to life. But first, I had to let go
of the past, which meant accepting that my life would never be the
same. I would never find the path back to "Larry and Sue." It dis-
appeared with him. But that didn't mean my journey was over. His
ending was simply my new beginning.

I've given up my permanent residence in *Grief World*, but I occasionally go back for a visit, just to regroup my thoughts and priorities
and to feel the love that surrounded me when Larry was alive. But
I never stay for long. I no longer belong there. I belong in the land
of the living – with all the people who loved and supported me as I
found a new road home.

Friends and Family: Caregivers for the Caregiver

It takes a lot of understanding, time,
and trust to gain a close friendship with someone.
As I approach a time of my life of
complete uncertainty,
my friends are my most precious asset.
~ERYNN MILLER~

Though our love story had a sad ending, Larry and I led a happy life together. We had so much for which to be grateful, but our biggest blessings were the people who became part of our story. Our family and friends made life beautiful and special for us, and after Larry's death, they made it bearable for me. Without them, I might never have found the strength to move forward.

When Larry got sick, cards and letters poured in from all over the world. Word of his illness spread through the networks of the people who loved him, and soon we were not only receiving well-wishes from friends and family, but from complete strangers – including leaders of churches in Asia and synagogues in the States, cancer survivors, friends of friends twice removed, employees of corporations based in other countries, and countless other people we'd never met. At no time in his final months did Larry feel neglected, forgotten, or unimportant to those in his world, nor did I.

At one point, Larry – who had always been practical, grounded, even stoic – told me that as soon as he was well again, he wanted to gather all of his friends in a park and have them hold hands and wrap their arms around each other so that he could express his love and gratitude for the light they brought to him. Of course, we never got to have that moment in what would have had to be a very large park, but I believe the hundreds of people who would have attended knew how he felt.

After Larry died, the support system we had formed proved invaluable to me. I would not have made it through the initial stages of my grief without the strength I found in the love and compassion of my friends and family.

In the beginning, there was a myriad of people offering their unconditional support, bringing food to my home, and calling or stopping by to check in and to distract me from loneliness. Hundreds showed up at the chapel to say their good-byes to Larry and to offer me their condolences. Many sent cards and flowers, and contributed to City of Hope and Hoag Hospital in Larry's name.

Eventually, the masses went back to their lives, but my closest friends were in it for the long haul. They bought groceries and put food in my refrigerator, or showed up with my favorite treats, without ever being asked. Several of them flew in or drove hundreds of miles on a regular basis just to show me they cared.

I was stubborn about asking for help, and most days I didn't want to see anyone anyway. I wanted to be alone to wallow in my misery. Those who were closest to me refused to accept no for an answer when I rejected their efforts. One particular couple, knowing that I was not doing well, called me one night and said they were coming over, whether I liked it or not. I was wrapped in a robe with fluffy slippers – my latest comfort outfit. They insisted I throw on something more appropriate and, within minutes, they were at my door with take-out food and disposable dinnerware. They quickly set my table, served the food, and even cleaned up afterward. Did I feel better? Yes. Did I cry that night? Yes, but it was different this time. Intermingled with the tears of pain and self-pity were tears of gratitude.

Of course, other friends eventually resumed their lives without making my grief their priority, tapering off slowly. That is the natural progression, and I was moved by earlier efforts. Then, there were other friends who had never been part of my daily life but yet continued to occasionally send notes or e-mails, or simply call. While I felt like the unluckiest woman in the world, I knew that I was also very fortunate.

Other friends faded away, though I admit that I was challenging to be around. In my self-absorption, which I still feel was warranted, I didn't consider the feelings of others, nor did I realize the mixed messages I was sending. I refused invitation after invitation, and almost lost friends as a result of not communicating clearly. One couple, who had been incredibly thoughtful and helpful before and during Larry's illness, finally told me to let them know when *I* was ready, and then stopped calling me. I felt abandoned and didn't realize for quite some time that my hurt and anger came from a somewhat selfish place.

A year later, I met my friend at a social event and confronted her with my hurt and disappointment. She explained that she had taken my recurring refusals as a message and was only trying to honor my wishes. I suddenly understood. Rift mended, friendship resumed, and a very major lesson learned.

To my surprise, I discovered that my daughters had similar experiences with their friends. They are fantastic women with fantastic people in their lives. They were overwhelmed by the kindness and love that many of their friends displayed when they lost their father. But others, to whom they had felt very close, disappointed them by not calling or being there for them as they expected. I don't think our family was alone in this experience. Sadly, it seems universal. As Dana said at the time, "Cream rises to the top."

I also think of friendship similar to a bull's-eye chart. The center is very small, the next concentric circle a little bigger, and so on until there are no more circles – or just circles I haven't yet explored. From this perspective, it's not so much about one friend being more helpful or reliable than another; everyone's just at a different level of familiarity, and that's okay.

Even with those closest to me, my grief sometimes made me a challenging friend. Two of my close friends finally told me to stop telling the world everything and to keep some things to myself. I have always been an open book. When I bump into people I know at the grocery store, and they ask how I am doing, I tell the truth – good or bad. I have always had this philosophy that if I hold something back, I'm not being honest. But because I was in a very negative place at this time, I wasn't always good company. I learned that most people don't want to know that your heart is tearing apart inside and that you want to run away. When the truth is that bad, and the listener is powerless to help, you're doing them a favor by saying you're fine.

A number of my friends also admitted that my life frightened them. None of them had lost their husbands, and my grief caused them to look at their lives and think about what they would do and how they would feel in my situation. They were distressed, not just for me, but also for themselves.

Still, they hung in there, even when I was repeating myself and spewing the negativity from which they could not save me. For the most part, they were kind enough to listen and to offer very little advice. And I appreciated that. I didn't want advice from anyone who hadn't lived through this.

As amazing as my friends were, it was my family that kept me from giving up. My daughters and sons-in-law were all grieving as well, but they still held me up when I was too weak and too low to stand on my own. They comforted me when their own eyes were brimming with tears and their bodies were shaking with fear and pain. They listened to my uncontrollable sobs, while holding back their own. And my grandchildren hugged me every chance they got, strengthening me with their smiles and laughter.

Though my daughters always stood by me, my grief made me hard for them to handle as well. They eventually became frustrated and hurt by my inability to be there for them – which is what a mother is supposed to do. They needed me, they said. They felt like they had lost both parents, because I was no longer present … not really. I was holed up inside my head, full of loneliness and misery.

I wish I could have been a better mother to them during this time. Both girls *adored* their father, and neither had as much experience with death as I did at their age. They needed me to provide support and reassurance that we would all be OK. They needed the strong, dependable, optimistic mother I had always been. But I was in such a dark place that I had no positive words, strength, or support to give. I couldn't even find those things for myself.

I couldn't think about what anyone else needed from me; I was simply doing my best to survive. Finally, I wrote a letter to both of them, attempting to apologize and offer hope that they would eventually have their mother back. Below are a few excerpts:

On the surface, and a little below, you view me as different from your mother circa 2008. So do I. That doesn't mean that what you see is what you'll get forever. It means that on my journey in this lifetime, I am right where I am supposed to be. What I am living is mine alone and no one can help me through the confusion, discovery, paths to explore, disappointments to endure, and lessons to learn. I have to work through the steps myself, and learn to pick myself up when I fall deeper than I thought was possible.

As I've said before, one of the huge lessons I have to learn in this lifetime is to give up wanting to always be the strong, controlling, dependable, self-sufficient one. I am finally learning to ask for help, and to accept it with gratitude, for as long as necessary. It's been a struggle, and remains that way, but it is one of my jobs at this time.

I have faith that this period is part of my journey, like all the others. I also have faith that when I emerge from this segment, I will be stronger, wiser, lighter, more sympathetic, and definitely more appreciative. I wish I could speed up the process or at least have an idea of the time frame, but neither of those are options.

Sharing too much with you has always been my weakness. I feel so close to both of you that too often I forget that a mother's role is not to add worry, fear, helplessness, and frustration to her children, no matter their age. Through this process of grieving, there is another life lesson for me to learn.

While I still feel guilty for the self-centered way in which I handled Larry's death, I have also discovered that it's important to be kinder to myself. My daughters lost one of the most important men in their lives. But I lost *the* most important man in mine – my husband, my best friend, the father of my children, my soul mate, my roommate, and my constant companion for 46 years.

This is not to say that their loss (or anyone's, for that matter) was less painful or real than mine – only that the loss of a spouse changes your life in ways that no other death could. And that change, that fear of the unknown, and that overwhelming loneliness is different from any other grief I've ever experienced.

With tragic exceptions, children usually outlive their parents. But when those children have built lives for themselves – have gotten married and perhaps had children of their own – they don't have the time to mourn themselves into a state of true depression and helplessness when they lose their parents. After all, they have other people counting on them. They have to continue making sure the kids get to school and dinners get made. They have to continue taking care of their families.

Losing a spouse is an entirely different matter. I had no husband or young children at home, counting on me to pull it together and care for them. My life had changed in every possible way, and I had nothing meaningful to distract me. I was alone with my grief.

And that was OK. Though my friends and family did not have the experience to join me in the kind of grief that only a widow knows, they never left my side. Even when they had no idea what to do with me, they held tightly to my hands, keeping me from drifting too far into the abyss.

As for Larry's gathering in the park, I did the next best thing. I gave a dinner party in his honor eight months after his passing, to thank the people who showed up to support me in my darkest hours. And though it was a tough night, where I and everyone else were looking around for Larry, it also helped me see a much-needed silver lining. Larry felt that way about his illness – that its unexpected blessing was the chance to see how many people loved him. His death gave me the same gift. During all of this, I never felt for one second that I was unloved or truly alone in this world.

Thanks to the undying support of my cherished friends and loved ones, Marilyn's deep wisdom, and the healing power of time, I eventually began to accept and embrace my new "normal."

My New "Normal"

Where you used to be, there is a hole in the world
which I find myself walking around in the daytime
and falling into at night. I miss you like hell.
~EDNA ST. VINCENT MILLAY~

A few years before Larry's death, we started a new Thanksgiving tradition. Instead of hosting dinner at our home for thirty or more guests, as we had done for decades, we began taking an intimate holiday getaway each year to either Hawaii or Mexico – with only each other, our daughters, and their families. In 2008, when we realized it wouldn't be wise for Larry to fly because of his immune system (or rather, lack thereof), we changed our reservations to a resort within driving distance. But Larry died just three weeks before Thanksgiving.

I was now the head of the family, a role I never wanted, and it was up to me to decide what to do for the holidays. Wanting to keep as much of our family life intact as possible, especially for the kids, I decided we would go anyway. The whole trip was a blur and so sad, but at least we were together.

It was hard from the first moments, when I was shown into the suite I had booked for "us." It echoed with emptiness. I broke down into uncontrollable hysterics. I couldn't, wouldn't, and didn't stay there. I gave the room to Dana and her family and took a regular room for myself.

When Larry and I traveled, we had almost always stayed in suites. This was the ultimate wake-up call. My life, which I had loved and treasured, would never be the same. This trip was supposed to help us maintain some sense of normality as a family. Instead, it drove home the realization that my "normal" life, the world I had been so comfortable and happy in, was a thing of the past.

In August, I decided to take our annual family photo – the first without Larry. Later, I would write in my journal:

Why, oh why, did I suggest this? It was so, so, so hard. Between shots, I kept running back into the house to wipe away the tears so I could smile for the next picture. My reality is that this is now my family. There is no Larry. But I want the kids to feel secure – to believe we'll all be OK and that we are still a strong, cohesive group. It's my feeble attempt at a future.

Larry's absence was not only felt on picture day; it also showed up in the photo. When the photographer showed me the proofs, I gasped. Though we had arranged ourselves in different positions and in front of different backgrounds, there was, in every picture, a noticeable space – a distinct chasm where another person should be. What was missing? We all knew.

Flash forward to a few years later, and I'm finding out that my new life – my new "normal" – isn't so bad. For the first year, I didn't travel much, at least not by my usual standards. I visited family in New York and San Francisco, took my grandsons and later my granddaughters for an overnight stay in a fun hotel, went with my daughters to our favorite spa in Arizona, and planned our annual Thanksgiving trip (the second without Larry).

The next year, I repeated the same trips but added a few additional destinations – including stays with dear friends in Carmel, Oregon, and the Berkshires, as well as a trip to New York to see my then-13-year-old grandson play in a baseball tournament and to visit my brother and sister-in-law.

Now, in my third year, I am pulling out my passport for the first time since losing Larry and taking my two oldest grandchildren to Italy – just the three of us. There's a lot of emotion attached to this trip. I never imagined I would be able to leave the country without Larry. We adored exploring the world, just the two of us. The thought of revisiting any place we enjoyed together seemed too painful and empty. Sure, I could travel with a friend. But no one would be as much fun as Larry. We anticipated each other's needs, protected each other, and enjoyed doing the same things. And going alone was out of the question. Although I had done it many times – to China, India, Australia, Egypt, France, and many other foreign countries – there was always some business associate to meet me, take me around, and try to woo my business. Travel without this security, and to be left for so long alone with my thoughts, would be overwhelming.

Then, last November, when the whole family was together in Hawaii for Thanksgiving, I told my grandkids that I really wanted to take them to Europe someday. And someone said, "Why not now?" Those words reverberated in my head. Yes, why *not* now? We all got excited. Bari immediately suggested Italy, and in that instant, it was a done deal. I could revisit all the places Larry and I had been together and share the adventures with his grandchildren. Their worshipped and adored Boppa would be with us, guiding us. He would be part of my explanations and anecdotes. What could be more wondrous?

I had dreaded the thought of stepping foot on foreign soil without Larry. Now, I can't wait to introduce my other four grandchildren to locations I visited with Larry in my other life. Like everything else, my readiness to travel came in time, as the new Sue – the solo act with a style all of her own – began to emerge.

A Picture of Sue Without Larry

If ever there is a tomorrow when we're not together,
there is something you must always remember. You are
braver than you believe, stronger than you seem, and
smarter than you think. But the most important thing
is, even if we're apart, I'll always be with you.
~A. A. MILNE, WINNIE THE POOH~

Earlier in this book, I reflected on the clichés people use to try and comfort us when we experience a great tragedy – sayings like, "He's in a better place now," "Time heals all wounds," and "This, too, shall pass." In the immediate aftermath of loss, these words seem hollow, even a bit irritating, and offer little comfort. But after some time has passed, and your head catches up to your broken heart, you just might find that there is wisdom and truth in some clichés.

The one I struggled with most was: "Everything happens for a reason." This is something I have always believed to be true, but losing Larry certainly tested my faith. What could possibly be the reason for Larry's death? He was a great man, who loved his family, friends, and community, who helped other people, who made the world a better place. And he didn't die saving another person's life or defending his country; he was slowly and painfully taken out of this world by his own body. I didn't see any *reason* in that, and the mere suggestion that there was one made me want to crawl back into my head, analyze, reanalyze, and try to make sense of a no-sense occurrence. But with a little time and a lot of help, I was eventually able to find my reason – and repair my bruised faith.

I have always felt there was something much larger than me, a force that showed itself in unexpected ways and validated that there was more to me than just a body and more to my life than a series of random events. As a child, I called it God. As a young adult, I questioned everything. As a mature woman with a little experience under her belt, I don't care what you call it. Call it the Universe, or God, or whatever, but I believe there is some sort of divine order with a hand in our fates and a purpose (or many purposes) for each of our lives.

I don't believe in coincidences. I have seen and experienced too much to believe in randomness – people who show up in our lives just when we need them, a book that jumps off the shelf at you when you need to read it most, or some other unexpected sign that helps point you in the right direction. This doesn't mean I don't have decisions to make or power to control outcomes, but it's not all haphazard – not in life, and not in death.

I've heard many theories about what happens after we die, but I have no insights or beliefs about the after-life. I don't believe in heaven or hell. But I can't accept that you just turn into ashes or dust, and nothing of you remains. I don't know what happens to our souls. Perhaps, they only continue to exist in the hearts of the people we leave behind. My husband gave part of himself to me, his children, and his grandchildren. He's incorporated into who we are – his beliefs, desires, thoughts, outlooks, values, and even his jokes.

I visit his grave often. It's in a beautiful park near the Pacific Ocean with no tombs or crumbling headstones. It's an easy place to be, and it's on my way home from almost everywhere. I sit on the ground next to his grave, beside the plot in which I will someday rest, and talk to him about what's going on in my life – sometimes aloud and sometimes just in my head. I don't know if he hears me but I like to think it's possible. And I'm OK with not knowing. After all, talking to him is more about comforting me than actually communicating with him. I guess you could say I don't know what I believe about any of it. But I do know that I am not just me. I have him with me, too.

This is, in part, what I had to learn before I could move past my grief – that there is always a reason, and that Larry is still a part of me. And for that lesson, I gratefully credit Shelly Eagle, a renowned "intuitive synergist" and a loving friend, who knew exactly what I needed to hear and gave me the words to move forward. Shelly helped me see that there was a simple reason for Larry's death: He had fulfilled his purpose in life, so it was time for him to go. I, however, was not finished with mine.

This understanding helped give me the courage to accept that I still had work to do in this world. My marriage to Larry was necessary for both of us. We learned so much from each other and strengthened each other in so many ways. But now I had my own lessons to learn and my own journey to take … this time, without him.

This part of my journey – redefining Sue without Larry – was a long, hard road. It took years to answer the questions that would allow me to be whole again: How could I define myself as a solo unit? Who was I … *really*? Who even wanted to know? How does one learn to feel complete without her other half?

Thankfully, I had a role model for strength and perseverance, someone who had inspired me with his determination for 46 years.

Larry had a sign on his desk which read: "When the wind stops, row." This perfectly captured the spirit of determination, resilience, and persistence that made Larry an inspiration to everyone who knew him … especially me. When he was gone, his faith and the confidence he always had in me continued to provide me with inspiration, as did the sign on his desk. When Larry died, the wind stopped. More realistically, the *world* stopped! And I knew that I had no choice but to row the boat myself.

With Shelly's help, I acknowledged that Larry had fulfilled his purpose in this lifetime. Larry was put here to complete his own journey and to show us the way. When his work was done, he passed on to the next place – but not without leaving a few parting gifts. For one thing, his death showed me how many people cared and loved me for myself. Shelly also encouraged me to think of the paperwork nightmare he left behind as a gift to me. It kept me so busy that I couldn't grieve 100 percent of the time. And by forcing me to organize our messy affairs – and then my messy life – he also showed me that I could do it, that I was strong enough.

You see, when you're with someone for nearly half a century, especially with someone as impressive as Larry, it's easy to forget your own strength. Much like his favorite literary character, Don Quixote, Larry was larger than life, an unstoppable force. But unlike Quixote, Larry's power and determination were based in reality and rationality, not imagination. Larry borrowed his motto from this windmill-chasing visionary – "to dream the impossible dream." Larry lived that dream, and he made it look easy.

This is not to say that I was ever the shy, humble "woman behind the man." I achieved much in my life and career. I was social, confident, smart, and influential in my own right. But in retrospect, I always saw him as the strong one, the powerhouse. And I felt lucky to be part of "Larry and Sue."

Without him, I am learning that it's not so bad just being Sue. In fact, it's pretty wonderful. While I would give it all up in a heartbeat to have him back, I am grateful to him for giving me the chance to chase my own windmills and to live my own impossible dream.

On the day that Larry's doctors conclusively told me that our 10-month battle with his cancer had been lost, and there was nothing more they could do, I struggled with the decision about whether to tell him. Larry's optimism had been so contagious that I had trouble letting it go. But I knew, just as I had known he was sick before the doctor ever said the word, that this was it. And he deserved to know.

When I told Larry that we had reached the point of no return, he said calmly, "So, it's not the end of a chapter. It's the end of the book."

These words have stuck with me over the years, and I have spent much time thinking about beginnings and endings. Yes, Larry's death was the end of a book – and the end of life as I knew it, as I planned it, as I wanted it. But, thanks to what I learned in the 46 years that I was part of his story, it was also a new beginning for me.

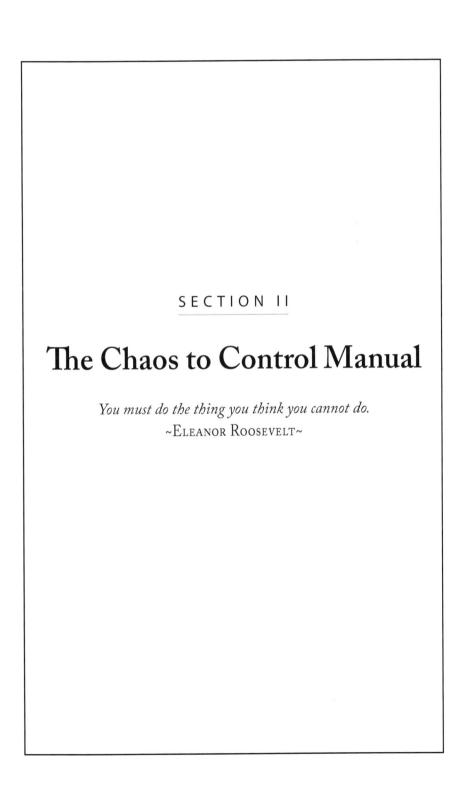

SECTION II

The Chaos to Control Manual

You must do the thing you think you cannot do.
~ELEANOR ROOSEVELT~

Drowning in Paperwork

Over the years, Larry and I both took on certain responsibilities in the running of our household. And for the most part, our financial affairs were his domain. This arrangement had nothing to do with my capabilities. While I was in the loop, and while we often made big decisions together, Larry *enjoyed* that particular chore, so I left that responsibility in his capable hands.

I paid some of the bills, and for those, I knew when they were coming, what to expect, and exactly what needed to be done. And I never paid much attention to the rest, because Larry had it under control. However, when he was in the hospital, many of the bills that usually landed on his desk were now suddenly on mine. For a while, it wasn't so bad. If I had questions, he could explain the back story and tell me what needed to be done.

Never, ever, could I have conceived of the monumental task this would become after Larry passed. I wasn't a woman whose husband took care of all the "big" aspects of our lives. I knew what we had and where it was. Even so, I didn't know what to do with it. Here I was, a successful, respected businesswoman, who had run several multi-million-dollar companies, and I had no idea what faced me with our personal finances. I can only imagine what it must be like for women who have never dealt with paperwork or money management at all.

It's no surprise that the poverty rates for single women over age 65 (about half of which are widows[1]) are some of the highest for any subgroup in the country[2], especially considering the fact that women are more than twice as likely to be widowed[3] and far less likely to have managed finances while their husbands were alive.

I literally dreaded the arrival of the mail. "How can two people generate so much paperwork?" I asked myself. "Who is this from? Did anyone ever hear of this company? Is this a mistake? How can they charge so much for that? Why don't the account numbers match? What do they want from me?"

As fast as I could reply to each letter, or call and speak to someone who was totally incapable of giving me the information I needed, another stack would arrive. I envisioned a future of endless telephone inquiries, of being chained to QuickBooks and credit card statements. Every time I solved a problem, another one (or two or five) would quickly fill the void.

At first, I loved Sundays and holidays, because there was no mail delivery. But I soon came to spend Sunday dreading the arrival of Monday, when the poor delivery man would hand me another stack of envelopes. It never stopped coming! Of course, it never will. When we die, our inboxes still won't be empty. But for someone walking around in a daze, barely able to perform such menial acts as showering or preparing meals, this was a nightmare.

I knew there was a myriad of things that needed my attention but had no idea what those things were. In addition to bills, there were government and financial agencies that needed to be notified,

---

1 U.S. Census Bureau

2 "Women and Social Security: Issue Brief." American Society of Actuaries. Washington, D.C., June 2007.

3 Kreider, Rose M. and Renee Ellis, "Number, Timing, and Duration of Marriages and Divorces: 2009." *Current Population Reports*, P70-125, U.S. Census Bureau, Washington, D.C., 2011.

paperwork that needed to be filed, legal documents that needed to be amended, insurance companies to deal with, and medical bills to resolve. But for much of this, I didn't know what I needed to do, by when, or even where to start. And how was I supposed to do this thing which required me to be focused, sharp, clear-minded, proactive, and capable of making wise decisions? I did not want to get out of bed in the morning, much less deal with notifying the bank, cancelling credit cards, listening to the attorney talk about exemption trusts, and discussing Form 706 with the accountant. This was important stuff, but I could barely hear the words coming out of their mouths. I just wanted it all to disappear.

As papers began accumulating, my dear friends Joanne and Myrna each flew in for a few days to help me get organized and to provide emotional support. We sorted through mail and put it all in files. OK, this was a good start ... until the next day, when more papers arrived, and there were more calls from the attorney, the insurance company, etc. All this occurred within the first few weeks, and I was grateful for the generous, loving support of my friends. But this was followed by several long and intense months when the work really began, and while I had plenty of people willing to help, there was no one to whom I could off-load the entire burden. It was mine.

The business part of my brain kicked into gear. There was no choice. Besides, I needed a distraction. There was no life for me other than my grief and paperwork. I knew there was nothing that would mellow the pain and despair, but the project of documentation and action could and needed to be handled. *That* I could control, which gave me the impetus to dig in and roll up my sleeves.

Please don't think I suddenly took on the world as a powerful, driven mogul. On the contrary, I spent weeks at a time in my home office, flitting from the computer to my files. I'd get up, shower, don sweats, have breakfast, and go into my office, often not emerging except for food, until midnight. It was tedious and overwhelming. Why hadn't anyone prepared a worksheet, a guideline, a manual of what I had to do and when? Why didn't I know what to expect?

In speaking with others who lost a significant person in their lives, I have come across a few I consider the truly lucky ones. These people had someone to take over their business of surviving – a brother, son, niece, grandchild, attorney, or advisor, someone who rolled up their sleeves, delegated, and completed tasks, and said, "OK, sign here." That signature would start the life insurance benefits, cancel policies, change over bank accounts, handle estate taxes, and pay bills. These survivors were overwhelmed with grief, but not with clerical duties. But as I've researched and talked with others who have gone through this, I have learned that the "lucky ones" are few and far between. Most people have to shake the cobwebs from their heads (as much as possible) and get it done. I was fortunate (in relative terms), as I was in both groups.

For more than forty years, Larry and I have been blessed with a close network of dear family friends ("second family" is probably more accurate). Howard Koff is one of these relatives we chose for ourselves. He was there for me as much as possible, especially in the beginning, when I needed him most. I was overwhelmed and bewildered, and his strength kept me from feeling that I was floating alone in another world. He helped me focus and avoid immediate panic by pointing me in the right direction.

A few weeks after Larry died, Howie met with my accountant, came to the house, looked over what, at first, seemed to be an orderly state of affairs, made some calls on my behalf, and scheduled a meeting with a group of financial advisors for us to interview together. It was an eye-opening experience. The information was all there, but instead of the well-ordered affairs I expected to see, I found a mess.

I cried and cried when they left, knowing that the task of sorting out the Pandora's box we had just opened would rest mainly in my lap. At least I now had an idea where to start, but my former attorney was not one to provide step-by-step direction, and my accountant at that time, although very caring and helpful, could only do so much.

Ultimately, that's what it boils down to. Others can't devote themselves fully to this project – and it does require devotion. People still have their own lives and day-to-day responsibilities, and as much as my family and friends wanted to help, they couldn't put their lives on hold for me indefinitely, nor would it have been fair for me to expect them to do so. But Howie had taught me an important lesson – to ask for, and accept help. I was grateful to him, and to the others who lent a hand, and when they needed to return to their own lives, I sought help in other ways.

I hired an assistant to help me with filing, sorting, and other tasks – a brilliant move! For the next year, I worked like that. But there was just too much I still didn't understand – business functions and jargon that were way outside my areas of expertise. And these things had to be done correctly, or they would come back to haunt me – and possibly jeopardize the financial stability that Larry and I had worked so hard to build for ourselves.

What I eventually discovered, after I crawled out of what seemed like a burial in paperwork, was that it started to lighten. And I found other people who could answer my questions and give me a hand. These individuals I lovingly and gratefully refer to as my team. They were respected professionals in their individual fields but didn't all know each other. That was easy to rectify. I connected all the people working with and for me, so they could work together in my interest. They enthusiastically agreed and proceeded to check back and forth with one another about what had been done, what was in the open file, and who would tackle the next project – while copying me on all e-mails and correspondence and informing me of other communications. I was completely in the loop, but not a go-between. They had their own language, which I'm sure was purposefully created to make us laymen feel inadequate. It worked. What were they saying? Whatever it was, I wasn't the cause of misinterpretation. Prior to that, I felt like a grade-school child playing telephone, not sure if the final message even resembled the original.

It took more than a year to put my team in place. In the meantime, I felt alone, confused, frustrated, and overwhelmed. I needlessly spent huge sums of money because I had no person or manual to assist me in thinking clearly and to prevent me from making costly mistakes. There had to be a better way to manage the logistics and business of personal loss. There is.

That's why I created the Chaos to Control program – to ensure that no one else has to go through what I went through … without any one-stop resource for getting her life back on track.

Each year, approximately 1.2 million Americans lose their spouses[4]. If you have recently become one of the club – a club I was literally welcomed into by another widow not long after Larry died – it helps to know you're not alone.

The loss of a spouse is a time of upheaval – emotionally, physically, psychologically, and mentally. I know from experience that, in the aftermath of loss, the grief and frustration make even the simplest of tasks seem overwhelming, and your life is currently far from simple. In addition to your usual responsibilities (full- or part-time work, managing a household, raising children, caring for aging relatives, etc.), you now have the additional weight of your partner's previous workload. And to top it off, you have the complicated task

---

4 Kreider, Rose M. and Renee Ellis, "Number, Timing, and Duration of Marriages and Divorces: 2009." *Current Population Reports*, P70-125. U.S. Census Bureau. Washington, D.C., 2011.

of getting your life back in order on paper. It's only natural to feel overwhelmed. Accept and respect that, in the midst of this new situation, you will feel less capable, less organized, less willing, and less grounded.

But you are not alone. In this section, I will guide you, step by step, through exactly what you need to do and when in order to get your estate organized and to plan for your future. If you follow the system, your work *will* be accomplished in an orderly, stress-reduced, and practical manner.

It's up to you – and as hard as it is to believe in the beginning, you can do it. But that doesn't mean you have to do everything yourself. In this section, you'll learn how to get your legal and accounting professionals working together on your behalf, which will save you a lot of stress. Of course, depending on how complicated and/or organized your affairs are, you may not need, or be able to afford, a team of professionals. But you probably have people in your life who want to help but have no idea how. In Section II, I suggest tasks that are perfect for delegating to friends or family members.

At the end of the day, you will emerge from the grief, even though this may seem impossible right now. And when you finally make it through the fear and uncertainty and believe that you can take control again, you become strong, powerful, confident, and proud. You realize that you can do it, whatever *it* may be. After all, you survived one of the worst tragedies a person can go through, but you're still alive and capable. Think of it as a chance to prove your mettle – if only to yourself.

PHASE 1

Getting Started

You've got a lot of work ahead of you, but it's important to remember that you don't have to do everything immediately. The Chaos to Control process breaks down the business of grief into small, manageable parts. The process is divided into three phases, each with its own steps – starting with the most urgent tasks.

In Phase 1, I will guide you through the three steps that *you must address now.* You will be working on these tasks simultaneously, so I highly recommend reading all of Phase 1 prior to beginning your work. The methodology will then be clear, and you can delve into each step with a strong foundation and a clear direction.

PHASE 1 STEPS

Step A: **Project Preparation and Organization**
Step B: **Immediate Notification**
Step C: **Self-Care**

Within each step, you'll learn what to do, how, and when. Let's get started.

Step A: Project Preparation and Organization

As you begin this process, you will face an onslaught of unexpected responsibilities, paperwork, and phone calls. You will need to locate, organize, prioritize, and act upon numerous documents. Allowed to pile up, these forms, bills, requests, and other paperwork will only add to the confusion and overwhelm you.

Tasks may seem insurmountable. It's essential that there be order. Your motto for this process is: Simplify. Organize. Move ahead.

Define Your Workspace

Start at the beginning: Where will you be working?

Designate a work area dedicated to this project only. If you're fortunate enough to have a home office, a den, a guest room, or any place that is not an integral part of your family's daily living space, this is the place to set up "Action Central."

If space is an issue, set up a portable or large folding table with moveable cartons or file boxes nearby.

Do not use your bedroom or kitchen as your workspace. These areas are part of your day-to-day life. These are places of your *present*. You need to sleep and eat without the constant reminder and distraction of this project. Your work may be sad. Let your present and past each have its own space.

Keep all of your office supplies in this area: pencils, pens, scissors, markers, notepads, stapler, stationery, envelopes, postage stamps, completed work, copies, etc. Having your work supplies readily available will save valuable time, effort, and energy.

Organize Your Project

Phone Calls and Conversations

Soon after your loss, you will need to speak with your attorneys, accountants, financial advisors, and banking institutions, and with the Social Security Administration to advise them of the situation. These are the immediate phone calls you will make and e-mails you will send, and you must keep accurate records. Detailed and organized guidance follows throughout the phase work.

When you are speaking with someone, make certain you ask what you must do to follow through. Have them repeat it. When possible, get it in writing. An e-mail or fax is as good as a hard copy.

Contacts at a Glance

Keep a contact binder near your telephone to record the dates, names, numbers, and relevant notes regarding all phone conversations. If you have signed up for one-on-one consulting with Susan Alpert Consulting, you have already received a contact book. If not, simply purchase a large, three-ring binder for this purpose.

This contact book is an essential resource that you will use often, and a great time-saver. This chronological listing makes it easy to identify at a glance with whom you spoke and when. Dedicate this binder to matters pertaining solely to the business aspects of your loss.

Later in this chapter, there is a worksheet designed to organize contact information for your selected Professional Team. (You can also download a copy to print and put in your binder at http://susanalpertconsulting.com/downloads/.) Keep this worksheet handy as well, so you will not have to hunt for phone numbers in the future. You can assemble this information as the need arises. It's not necessary to do this in advance.

Finally, keep all relevant business cards in one place. You can purchase plastic, divided sheets for this purpose.

Receipts

Keep your receipts! Many expenses associated with your

organizational work can be reimbursed (via the estate) or itemized and deducted on your tax return. Costs associated with documentation (e.g., photocopying, postage, and mileage) should be closely documented, as well as records and receipts relating to funeral expenses.

Check with your legal and tax advisors for current rules and regulations, and to discuss whether you qualify for these write-offs.

Set Up the Filing System

You need a paper system for the ensuing work, and perhaps you already have one. Most likely, because your loss is new, you haven't yet established this system. Now is the time. Following the guidelines of the system below, you will create a plan or refine your existing one.

Identify and Access

This methodology is designed to make it as simple as possible to quickly identify and access your critical documentation and notes. If you are using your personal system, the most important consideration is that you know where everything is located and that you can easily access information. If you have signed up for a one-on-one consultation with Susan Alpert Consulting, you have already received a starter kit with the materials needed to create the filing system outlined below. If not, you can purchase what you need at any office supply store.

Here are the basics:

- 20 to 30 manila file folders (referred to below as *files*)
- One red file folder and one blue file folder (referred to below as *status files)*
- 10 multi-colored expanding file folders (referring to below as *folders)*
- A filing area, or portable boxes

The system is color-coded to help you immediately identify the status of your documents, process, and project. Your color-coded folders are divided by category. This organized and segmented filing system will serve as the "main brain" for your project work.

Getting organized is a big step, and it's challenging work. But being able to easily put your hands on important documentation helps reduce your stress and overall anxiety. The more organized you are, the more smoothly the project will run.

Using Folders and Files

There are two parts to the system: *Organizational* files and *Status* files.

ORGANIZATIONAL FILES

Organizational files contain all the paper-based documentation that you will gather during your project. It consists of alphabetical, color-coded *folders* that contain individual *files*.

Think of this filing system like a department store. In the Appliances Department, there are aisles for different types of products, such as dishwashers, cook-tops, and refrigerators. Likewise, your Insurance folder contains files for different types of products, such as life, health, and auto policies. And just as the refrigerator aisle contains numerous individual manufacturers or models, your Auto Insurance file may contain individual sub-files for multiple insurers or vehicles.

Your Organizational filing system may include, but will not be limited to, the following folders:

- Accounting
- Banking (checking, savings, safe deposit box accounts, etc.)
- Financial Investments (financial, real estate, art, collections, etc.)

- Government and Civil
- Insurance
- Legal

These top-level categories (*folders*) provide an umbrella for information from individual providers and institutions (*files*). This structure will become clearer as you work with it.

Example: You'll have a colored, expandable folder for Banking. Within that folder you will need separate manila files for each banking institution, and then sub-files dedicated to each account held at each institution. Sub-files will include items such as safe deposit box statements, completed bank forms, monthly checking statements, etc. You may also need to segment personal and business accounts.

The same hierarchy holds for all of your service providers and institutions (legal, accounting, financial, property, insurance, credit cards, etc.). In addition to our list above, you may have separate and unique categories to consider.

Each top-level *folder* is a different color. Each *file* and sub-file is plain manila. Sub-files may be differentiated with different colored labels or by other means.

Sorting: At this point, it's not necessary to hone in on small details. In fact, it's very important *not* to get hung up on the details. Simply place the appropriate papers you have gathered or received into the correct folders. Detailed sorting will automatically happen as you work within the categories.

Labeling: Don't forget to label each folder and file. Use what works for you: handwritten, computer-printed, or P-touch labels.

STATUS FILES

Two Status files – individual, colored files that are separate from the category folders and files – help you manage the work in progress:

- **Blue:** Waiting for Response (pending communications)
- **Red:** Action Needed (communication/tasks that require your attention)

Keep your Status files handy. At a glance, you can see what's yours to do and what you're waiting for someone else to do. Check the "Waiting for Response" (blue) file weekly to make sure nothing falls through the cracks while you focus on your red folder items.

Ask for Help

Establishing and labeling your filing system may be a good project to delegate. A friend, family member, or assistant can shop for the materials (and other office supplies) and set up the system. Save your energy for things that only you can do.

Incoming Mail

Incoming mail is the source of most household clutter. Go through your mail daily. Keep or toss right away.

Dump the junk. Discard and recycle obvious junk mail, unwanted magazines, circulars, etc. This immediately clears the mess and frees space in your work area ... and your head.

Sort. Carefully sort each piece of mail into two stacks:

Stack 1: Immediate attention. Separate the items that need your immediate attention and action. You'll probably recognize them as they arrive: credit card statements, bills, legal documents, etc.

Stack 2: Open and prioritize. Don't neglect this second stack. These items need to be opened in a timely fashion (within the business week), but they are *not urgent*.

Bills need to be paid as soon as possible. However, if something slips through the cracks for a few weeks, there is very little likelihood that your services (e.g., utilities) will be discontinued immediately. You may incur late fees on overdue items, but in the long run, this is a minor annoyance.

Keep a paper trail of all billing and other pertinent mail for at least four months. This will be a vital thread and record of the business you need to handle. It's an insight into the deceased person's life and provides another checklist of things you need to handle.

Murphy's Law will at some point come into play; something will go missing. If you can't locate it, never knew about, or have no idea what it is – chances are, it's in your mailbox. It may not show up now, but be on the lookout in the future. There are always surprises.

Acknowledge Your Progress

Once you start to organize and get a good sense of the scope of the work ahead of you, you may wonder how you will handle everything. At a time when it's essential to be focused and proactive, your grief, compounded by your personal and financial concerns, may seem overpowering. Know that you have taken the most important step: You have started the journey. You will get it done.

Step B: Immediate Notification

You got organized in Step A. That preparation lays the foundation. Now, it's time to get things moving. I've created a hierarchy of things to do, and people and organizations to contact. This step-by-step guide will help you manage the process so that you're not overwhelmed by the sheer number of communications associated with personal loss.

Whom do you call first? Start with the most important. **This is your A-list:**

- Your Professional Team
- Insurance
- Social Security

Your Professional Team

First things first: Notify your Professional Team of your loss and life changes.

The make-up of this team will vary dramatically from person to person. Everyone's legal and financial situation is different. Your Professional Team could include attorneys, financial advisors, brokers, accountants, insurance agents, and other professional service providers. If your estate is complicated (e.g., if you have investments in different places, legal matters that need to be resolved, etc.), you'll want some or all of these people working in your corner.

If your affairs are less complicated, and/or if you don't have the resources to hire professionals, you still need people who are thinking more clearly than you at the moment and who would be willing to take some of the tasks off your plate. Do you have any family members or close friends (preferably those with some experience in this area) who would be willing to work together on your behalf? If so, now is the time to reach out.

Once you have everyone on board, it's time to get them connected and collaborating on your behalf. Chances are, the members of your Professional Team do not know one another. Now is the time for introductions.

Contact each of your advisors and explain your "My Team" philosophy. Communicate that you value their expertise and that you need their help as you work through the Chaos to Control process. Ask if they will speak to and work directly with your other team members, and then send the Professional Team contact list to all of them.

When your team members work directly with one another, it saves you time, money, and aggravation. You don't need to be the go-between or the interpreter. Your project work will be more accurate, the team will work more efficiently, and each player will feel a greater responsibility to act on your behalf. Not only are they accountable to you, they are also now accountable to each other to get things done.

While they will work one-on-one or together, you still need to be in the loop. Ask your team to copy you on all correspondence and to inform you of any other communications on your behalf.

Earlier, we discussed keeping records of important contacts. Fill out the worksheet entitled "A-List Contacts" at the end of Phase 1, and get those business cards into the plastic sheets. Having the contact information for your team in one place is a huge time- and stress-saver, as you will probably refer to this resource frequently.

If some of this information is not readily available, now is the time to locate and gather it.

Insurance

Is there insurance? This is one of the first questions asked after a loss, and for a vital reason. If you don't already know what you have, find out immediately so that you can file the appropriate claims and receive your compensation, if applicable.

Acquiring this information should be part of the discovery process and is another great job to assign a family member or friend. No matter who ultimately ends up with the task, someone should search drawers, computer files, and desks for policies or contact information for insurance agents. Also, contact any known insurance agents, attorneys, unions, or employers (even if the deceased is retired, as he/she may have a pension fund with life insurance benefits). Generally, one of these sources will have information on any insurance that might exist.

If you're fortunate, you may have only one or two brokers handling all your policies. But you may have multiple carriers, which can get complicated. The worksheets at the end of this Phase provide a guideline to the types of policies in a typical estate.

This is extremely important and time-sensitive. You'll want to receive any payments due to you or other beneficiaries from the deceased's estate as soon as possible. And you'll need to amend your own policies (if the deceased was your beneficiary).

Most companies are very responsive, but sometimes there can be a delay, so start this process quickly. After the initial contact, you will have to complete the following:

File claims or make amendments. File claims with or submit updates to all the companies. There may be several policies in addition to individual life insurance. Some other types of policies that provide death benefits include the following:
- Association-sponsored
- Casualty
- Credit card- and bank-sponsored
- Employer- and union-sponsored
- Group life
- Health and accident

- Mortgage
- Property (homeowners, renters, business)
- Travel
- Veterans Administration

Frequently, individuals have multiple policies through a broker or through one or two major insurers. Check with these providers first. Make certain that your files are up to date, your personal records in order, and your checklists current.

Cancel or amend other policies, including:
- Automobile
- Health (if the deceased had policies not sponsored by his/her employer)
- Long-term life (you may be entitled to receive credit for any unused portion of the annual payment)
- Personal/umbrella

Social Security

If you have not already notified the Social Security Administration of your loss, do so immediately. (Note: In some cases, the funeral home will already have done this on your behalf, so you may want to ask the funeral director before you call.)

First, gather the following information:
- Deceased's Social Security Number
- Deceased's Date of birth
- Date of marriage (if applicable)

Then, call the Social Security Administration at (800) 772-1213. They will tell you what you need to do. Don't be afraid to ask questions and to ask for clarification.

Remember to write down these details in your contact binder:
- Date of the conversation
- Information and instructions
- Name of the person with whom you spoke

In the future, you will need these documents:
- Birth certificate
- Marriage certificate (if applicable)
- Birth certificates of any dependent children
- Copies of the deceased's most recent federal tax returns

Federal Benefits

If your spouse has been receiving federal benefits, and if you are also old enough to receive those benefits, you are entitled to the larger amount: either 50 percent of your spouse's allowance or 100 percent of yours. To claim spousal benefits, you'll need a copy of your marriage certificate.

Regardless of age, a spouse may also claim a $255 one-time payment by filing a claim with the Social Security Administration. You have two years after the death to submit this request.

In individual circumstances, children who are under the age of 18 or are disabled may also be entitled to benefits. Again, check with your local agency.

Disclaimer: Susan Alpert Consulting has, to the best of its ability, verified the accuracy of all advice within the Chaos to Control process. As with all tax and financial recommendations, please check with all the members of your Professional Team for current changes to the laws and processes.

Step C: Self-Care

Steps A and B have involved a great deal of mental, physical, and emotional work. Please remember, during this process and beyond, it is vital to take care of yourself.

You may have children, aging parents, or other people depending on you. We all know that in order to care for others, we have to take care of ourselves. That's why flight attendants tell us that, in case of emergency, we should secure our own oxygen masks before those of our children.

But there's a difference between *knowing* and *doing.* And when we're stressed, anxious, and grieving, the *knowing* often goes out the window – which often means we *don't* do for ourselves.

Put Yourself First

It's too easy to push ourselves and our well-being to the bottom of our to-do lists. Actually, now is the time to put *you* first. You will need all your strength and stamina just when you're at your weakest.

Slow Down

Acknowledge that you can't do everything at once. Don't rush. Be kind to yourself and limit your expectations. Resist the urge to be impulsive. You've probably heard the old adage that it's wise not to make any major changes in the first year after a personal crisis. This has proven to be true again and again. You may regret rushed decisions after you've had some time to settle into your new life. Listen closely to the advice of your trusted Professional Team and pace yourself.

Accept and Ask for Help

Family and friends truly want and *need* to help you. So, let them.

Consider it as much a favor for them as for you. People often don't know what to say to a grieving person. The people who love you probably feel helpless and uncomfortable. They want to be there for you, but they're not sure what you need or how to help. Reach out. If you need a ride, a meal, someone to make phone calls or write letters, anything – just ask.

And accept help. When people who care about you offer assistance, say yes and tell them exactly how they can make life easier for you. Don't just say you're "fine." You're not, and you're not supposed to be yet.

As discussed earlier, you may want to consider having someone to work alongside you for a while. This trusted person could be a relative, a dear friend, a professional organizer, or an assistant. You need someone to help relieve some of the responsibility of these mundane but necessary tasks. In the long run, it will make your life and this process easier.

Go Pro

Professional grief counselors and facilitated support groups are widely available. They understand what you are experiencing and can be immensely helpful during this personally challenging period.

Susan Alpert Consulting can provide clients with local referrals, but a wealth of information and help is available through hospitals, hospices, public health agencies, senior citizen groups, churches, and the Veterans Administration, to name just a few.

One of the best places to start is with your doctor, who can address any physical symptoms you are experiencing and direct you to additional mental health resources. You can also ask friends and family members for referrals, or search online and in the telephone directory under "mental health," "grief support," "bereavement," and similar listings.

Especially if you have been a longtime caregiver before your loss, support at this time is critical.

Get Outdoors

Try walking, exercising, visiting, shopping, anything that will get you out of the house for a little while. Getting out will not only help to refresh your mind, but will be a gift to your body as well. Walking as few as 15 or 20 minutes a day, or seeing friends or family a few times a week, makes a measurable difference in your well-being and outlook, and is an important part of your transition process.

It's natural to want to stay under the covers, but don't sequester yourself at home. You're there enough. Although it may require great effort and, for a while, you might even dread seeing the people you love most, taking that break is a vital step in moving forward.

Eat Regularly and Well

This may be difficult for some people and easy for others. It depends on your relationship with food during times of stress. Regardless, a well-balanced diet is essential.

This doesn't necessarily mean that you must eat three square meals every day. Just be aware that your body will rebel if it's not nourished with a well-balanced selection of lean proteins, complex carbohydrates, healthy fats, minerals, and vitamins. And the last thing you need right now is to get sick. You need every advantage you can get as you work through this process – and through your grief.

A simple rule of thumb is to try to have a colorful plate with something from all the food groups. Easy? Not always. Worth the effort? Definitely.

Avoid alcohol, excessive caffeine, and drugs (other than those prescribed by your doctor; and take those only as directed). These will only dehydrate you, add to your exhaustion, and complicate your emotions.

Be kind to yourself. If you've eaten something that's not on the "healthy and good-for-you" list, take a breath and relax. Burgers and ice cream have their place. Don't punish yourself. Do try to be aware of what you're eating, when, and why. Balance will come.

Get Sleep

Stress may impact your ability to sleep soundly. You may be unable to fall or stay asleep, or you may simply feel perpetually fatigued. Whatever you feel, respect yourself. Your immune system must stay strong to tolerate the pressure and disruptions of your personal situation. Every part of you needs restorative sleep: your body and your mind. If you experience ongoing sleep difficulty, contact your doctor, who may recommend relaxation techniques, or prescribe sleep aids or other medication during this period.

Stress impacts health in general. If a condition worsens, or you develop new health issues, see your doctor.

Take a Break

You may not think you have time to rest because of everything you have to do. But adding a little breathing room in your schedule actually improves your productivity, progress, and outlook. Put "breaks" on your to-do list ... every day.

There are many ways to rest:
- Move to a room that is not dedicated to work
- Put your feet up
- Read
- Listen to music
- Get a massage

- Take a short nap
- Go for a walk
- Meditate
- Take a yoga class

An individual's respite is personal. Do whatever gives you more stamina and focus when you return to your responsibilities.

You Will Be OK

Reread these reminders when you're stressed, tired, overwhelmed, or stuck in your process. This is your time to re-imagine, reconfigure, and redefine your life.

Give yourself your attention and your care. The better you feel, the more capable you will be.

Congratulations!

You've taken the first big step in moving from Chaos to Control: Your project is organized. You have notified the most important individuals and organizations. Your team and other key contacts have been identified, and their contact information resides in one, easy-to-locate place. Take a deep breath; you've done good work.

Now, you're ready to take additional positive and productive action and begin Phase 2 of the Chaos to Control process: Assessment.

To download the worksheets online, please visit my site, http://susanalpertconsulting.com/downloads/.

Ask for Help

The worksheet may look formidable, but it's an excellent task to delegate to a relative, trusted friend, or professional organizer.

Phase 1 Worksheets

A-List Contacts

LEGAL	Attorney 1
Firm Name:	
Attorney Name:	
Address:	
Telephone:	
Fax:	
E-mail:	
Assistant Name:	
Telephone:	
E-Mail:	
Notes:	

LEGAL	Attorney 2
Firm Name:	
Attorney Name:	
Address:	
Telephone:	
Fax:	
E-mail:	
Assistant Name:	
Telephone:	
E-Mail:	
Notes:	

FINANCIAL	Personal Accountant
Firm Name:	
Accountant Name:	
Address:	
Telephone:	
Fax:	
E-mail:	
Assistant Name:	
Telephone:	
E-Mail:	
Notes:	

FINANCIAL	Business Accountant
Firm Name:	
Accountant Name:	
Address:	
Telephone:	
Fax:	
E-mail:	
Assistant Name:	
Telephone:	
E-Mail:	
Notes:	

FINANCIAL	Financial Advisors 1
Firm Name:	
Advisor Name:	
Address:	
Telephone:	
Fax:	
E-mail:	
Assistant Name:	
Telephone:	
E-Mail:	
Notes:	

FINANCIAL	Financial Advisors 2
Firm Name:	
Advisor Name:	
Address:	
Telephone:	
Fax:	
E-mail:	
Assistant Name:	
Telephone:	
E-Mail:	
Notes:	

FINANCIAL	Financial Advisors 3
Firm Name:	
Advisor Name:	
Address:	
Telephone:	
Fax:	
E-mail:	
Assistant Name:	
Telephone:	
E-Mail:	
Notes:	

NOTE:

Life insurance policies vary greatly. Your loved one may have had individual policies, and/or those sponsored by employers, associations, credit cards, banks, or charitable organizations. The policies may be further subcategorized by whole or term, separate trust, etc.

LIFE INSURANCE	Life Insurance Policy No. 1
Company Name:	
Policy Number:	
Name on Policy:	
Date of Birth:	
Beneficiary(ies):	1. 2. 3.
Contact Name:	
Telephone:	
Fax:	
E-Mail:	
Notes:	

LIFE INSURANCE	**Life Insurance Policy No. 2**
Company Name:	
Policy Number:	
Name on Policy:	
Date of Birth:	
Beneficiary(ies):	1. 2. 3.
Contact Name:	
Telephone:	
Fax:	
E-Mail:	
Notes:	

LIFE INSURANCE	Life Insurance Policy No. 3
Company Name:	
Policy Number:	
Name on Policy:	
Date of Birth:	
Beneficiary(ies):	1. 2. 3.
Contact Name:	
Telephone:	
Fax:	
E-Mail:	
Notes:	

LIFE INSURANCE	Life Insurance Policy No. 4
Company Name:	
Policy Number:	
Name on Policy:	
Date of Birth:	
Beneficiary(ies):	1. 2. 3.
Contact Name:	
Telephone:	
Fax:	
E-Mail:	
Notes:	

LONG TERM CARE INSURANCE	Long Term Care Insurance Policy No. 1
Company Name:	
Policy Number:	
Name on Policy:	
Date of Birth:	
Beneficiary(ies):	1. 2. 3.
Contact Name:	
Telephone:	
Fax:	
E-Mail:	
Notes:	

CASUALTY INSURANCE	Casualty Insurance Policy No. 1
Company Name:	
Policy Number:	
Name on Policy:	
Date of Birth:	
Beneficiary(ies):	1. 2. 3.
Contact Name:	
Telephone:	
Fax:	
E-Mail:	
Notes:	

CASUALTY INSURANCE	Casualty Insurance Policy No. 2
Company Name:	
Policy Number:	
Name on Policy:	
Date of Birth:	
Beneficiary(ies):	1. 2. 3.
Contact Name:	
Telephone:	
Fax:	
E-Mail:	
Notes:	

CASUALTY INSURANCE	Casualty Insurance Policy No. 3
Company Name:	
Policy Number:	
Name on Policy:	
Date of Birth:	
Beneficiary(ies):	1. 2. 3.
Contact Name:	
Telephone:	
Fax:	
E-Mail:	
Notes:	

PERSONAL INSURANCE	Personal Insurance Policy No. 1
Company Name:	
Policy Number:	
Name on Policy:	
Date of Birth:	
Beneficiary(ies):	1. 2. 3.
Contact Name:	
Telephone:	
Fax:	
E-Mail:	
Notes:	

PERSONAL INSURANCE	Umbrella Insurance Policy No. 1
Company Name:	
Policy Number:	
Name on Policy:	
Date of Birth:	
Beneficiary(ies):	1. 2. 3.
Contact Name:	
Telephone:	
Fax:	
E-Mail:	
Notes:	

PERSONAL INSURANCE	Umbrella Insurance Policy No. 2
Company Name:	
Policy Number:	
Name on Policy:	
Date of Birth:	
Beneficiary(ies):	1. 2. 3.
Contact Name:	
Telephone:	
Fax:	
E-Mail:	
Notes:	

PROPERTY INSURANCE	Property Insurance Policy No. 1
Company Name:	
Policy Number:	
Name on Policy:	
Date of Birth:	
Beneficiary(ies):	1. 2. 3.
Contact Name:	
Telephone:	
Fax:	
E-Mail:	
Notes:	

PROPERTY INSURANCE	Property Insurance Policy No. 2
Company Name:	
Policy Number:	
Name on Policy:	
Date of Birth:	
Beneficiary(ies):	1. 2. 3.
Contact Name:	
Telephone:	
Fax:	
E-Mail:	
Notes:	

MORTGAGE INSURANCE	Mortgage Insurance Policy No. 1
Company Name:	
Policy Number:	
Name on Policy:	
Date of Birth:	
Beneficiary(ies):	1. 2. 3.
Contact Name:	
Telephone:	
Fax:	
E-Mail:	
Notes:	

MORTGAGE INSURANCE	Mortgage Insurance Policy No. 2
Company Name:	
Policy Number:	
Name on Policy:	
Date of Birth:	
Beneficiary(ies):	1. 2. 3.
Contact Name:	
Telephone:	
Fax:	
E-Mail:	
Notes:	

BUSINESS INSURANCE	Business Insurance Policy No. 1
Company Name:	
Policy Number:	
Name on Policy:	
Date of Birth:	
Beneficiary(ies):	1. 2. 3.
Contact Name:	
Telephone:	
Fax:	
E-Mail:	
Notes:	

BUSINESS INSURANCE	Business Insurance Policy No. 2
Company Name:	
Policy Number:	
Name on Policy:	
Date of Birth:	
Beneficiary(ies):	1. 2. 3.
Contact Name:	
Telephone:	
Fax:	
E-Mail:	
Notes:	

VALUABLES INSURANCE	Valuables Insurance Policy No. 1
Company Name:	
Policy Number:	
Name on Policy:	
Date of Birth:	
Beneficiary(ies):	1. 2. 3.
Contact Name:	
Telephone:	
Fax:	
E-Mail:	
Notes:	

VALUABLES INSURANCE	Valuables Insurance Policy No. 2
Company Name:	
Policy Number:	
Name on Policy:	
Date of Birth:	
Beneficiary(ies):	1. 2. 3.
Contact Name:	
Telephone:	
Fax:	
E-Mail:	
Notes:	

AUTOMOBILE INSURANCE	Automobile Insurance Policy No. 1
Company Name:	
Policy Number:	
Name on Policy:	
Contact Name:	
Telephone:	
Fax:	
E-Mail:	
Notes:	

AUTOMOBILE INSURANCE	Automobile Insurance Policy No. 2
Company Name:	
Policy Number:	
Name on Policy:	
Contact Name:	
Telephone:	
Fax:	
E-Mail:	
Notes:	

AUTOMOBILE INSURANCE	Automobile Insurance Policy No. 3
Company Name:	
Policy Number:	
Name on Policy:	
Contact Name:	
Telephone:	
Fax:	
E-Mail:	
Notes:	

OTHER VEHICLE INSURANCE (Boat, RV, Motorcycle)	Other Vehicle Insurance Policy No. 1
Company Name:	
Policy Number:	
Name on Policy:	
Contact Name:	
Telephone:	
Fax:	
E-Mail:	
Notes:	

OTHER VEHICLE INSURANCE (Boat, RV, Motorcycle)	Other Vehicle Insurance Policy No. 2
Company Name:	
Policy Number:	
Name on Policy:	
Contact Name:	
Telephone:	
Fax:	
E-Mail:	
Notes:	

OTHER VEHICLE INSURANCE (Boat, RV, Motorcycle)	Other Vehicle Insurance Policy No. 3
Company Name:	
Policy Number:	
Name on Policy:	
Contact Name:	
Telephone:	
Fax:	
E-Mail:	
Notes:	

TRAVEL INSURANCE	Travel Insurance Policy No. 1
Company Name:	
Policy Number:	
Name on Policy:	
Date of Birth:	
Beneficiary(ies):	1. 2. 3.
Contact Name:	
Telephone:	
Fax:	
E-Mail:	
Notes:	

TRAVEL INSURANCE	Travel Insurance Policy No. 2
Company Name:	
Policy Number:	
Name on Policy:	
Date of Birth:	
Beneficiary(ies):	1. 2. 3.
Contact Name:	
Telephone:	
Fax:	
E-Mail:	
Notes:	

VETERANS ADMINISTRATION (VA) INSURANCE	VA Insurance Policy
Company Name:	
Policy Number:	
Name on Policy:	
Date of Birth:	
Beneficiary(ies):	1. 2. 3.
Contact Name:	
Telephone:	
Fax:	
E-Mail:	
Notes:	

PHASE 2

Assessment

Perhaps the biggest obstacle you will face as you work through the logistics of your loss is that you don't know what you don't know. That's where things fall through the cracks, and you end up redoing tasks. You may start to question your competence. This is only natural, but be kind to yourself and remember that you have probably never done this before, and it's not an easy job. Again, that's exactly why this manual was created.

You've accomplished a lot already! In Phase 1, you organized your project, notified critical agencies and individuals, and began steps to take care of yourself.

Now, the true, hands-on work starts. Taken one section at a time, trusting that each piece will fall into place (you'll put it there), and the work will get done.

PHASE 2 STEPS

Step A: Define Your Process
Step B: B-List Provider Notification and Update
Step C: Document Discovery

In Phase 1, you worked with your A-List providers: your team, insurance carriers, and the Social Security Administration – all of whom should have set things in motion. Now, it's time to move on to the second group of providers – your B-List and everyone else who must be contacted.

Step A: Define Your Process

The manner in which you receive and store your documentation will define the way you access your information in this and all subsequent work. Stay in your comfort zone. If you're a paper-based person, now may not be the best time to try to learn a lot of new technology. Which description fits you best?

Paper: If you run a mostly paper-based household and business, then your documents should be generally accessible to anyone who can sort through hard-copy files, folders, stacks, and boxes.

Electronic: If some or all of your documentation is received and stored electronically – perhaps on a home or business computer – then you'll need passwords to access your critical information. Remember that you may need access to information on other electronic devices, such as smartphones (BlackBerry, iPhone, Android) or tablets (iPad, Xoom). You'll need e-mail passwords as well as passwords for online accounts. Electronic documents may include – but are not limited to – banking and investment statements, tax records, e-mail correspondence, and receipts. Keep passwords in a safe place.

Tech Help

If you're not technologically savvy or dexterous – or are simply overwhelmed – trustworthy tech help is available. Reputable companies such as the Geek Squad and Make It Work support individual clients on password issues, document access, and ongoing technology support.

Step B: B-List Provider Notification and Update

Many companies, organizations, and agencies must be notified of your loss. During this phase, I will help you define and prioritize which additional agencies to contact and when.

You'll need to notify each provider of your loss, and update your accounts and records to reflect your current status (account holder, beneficiaries, etc.).

Depending on the agency or institution, you may update an account through hard-copy correspondence, e-mail, PDF, website, fax, or phone. In some cases, you'll create and submit a form letter.

Please check with each agency, specifically, to verify its process – and then adhere to it.

Begin with Statements

Start your Phase 2 notification work with the monthly and quarterly bills and statements that you receive. These usually contain account numbers, balances, and other pertinent information. It's easiest to begin here, because you'll be receiving these papers by mail or electronically, and you can stay current as they arrive.

For example, a brokerage account statement will include all of the following:

- Agency representative and contact information (telephone/e-mail)
- Account number
- Type of account
- Date of last monthly, quarterly, or annual statement

If you pay your bills with a hard-copy check (versus online bill-pay), be sure to note your account update(s) on the return portion of the statement.

Prioritize Payments

The sheer volume of paperwork you're dealing with can be overwhelming. Remember, not everything is urgent. However, a few things do need to be addressed in a timely manner: bills.

Make certain to first pay all outstanding bills and continue to do so as they arrive. If you've established automatic bill-pay, note the date the payment is due, and send a letter to the billing company informing them of your account changes.

For tips on how to manage your incoming mail, refer to pages 77-78 in Phase 1, which provides a guide to help you figure out what to keep, toss, or deal with, and when.

Remember to keep copies of everything you send. Place copies of items that will be receiving a response into your blue "Waiting for Response" Status file. Anything that will not generate a response may be filed in the appropriate Organizational file folder.

You do not need to alert everyone or every agency at this time – just those identified as most critical now.

[See the worksheet "B-List Providers Checklist," page 141.]

Get Professional Advice

Again, listen to the advice of your professionals. Your Professional Team members may be handling some of these notifications for you or may have other instructions based on your individual situation.

Remind Yourself You're Healing

The grief and upheaval you're experiencing are part of an ongoing healing process. You need to move through each stage to come out on the other side a more capable person.

Don't expect too much of yourself. And don't expect too much too quickly. This all takes time.

Do what you can without sacrificing your well-being.

Life's in-box is never empty. There will always be items to handle, but not all at the same time. You will get it all done.

Step C: Document Discovery

As you venture forward, you will be collecting a myriad of documents and facing unexpected tasks. The following Document Discovery and Status Checklist will familiarize you with the challenges ahead and remove the trepidation of the unknown. It will also acquaint you with terms and categories that may be new or unexplored.

At first glance, the list may seem long and impossible to complete. Because it covers most of the minute details, divided into smaller segments, it actually will make the process of gathering these items easier for you.

Remember, you're not supposed to know all this yet. Some of these items you have never handled, have forgotten, or have had no previous need to know. The checklist is segmented into four categories:

- Government and Civil Documents
- Legal Documents
- Financial Documents – Assets
- Financial Documents – Liabilities

The steps you take to gather these documents require effort, energy, and attention to detail – something you may not feel that you have right now. But with each document you locate, you will be closer to your goal of establishing an organized framework. You'll gain a greater understanding of your situation (current and future), and the tasks will eventually be simpler and less daunting.

You already prepared color-coded folders to house the documents you're collecting. Make sure that each time you find, handle, or act upon a document, you place it in its proper folder, readily accessible for the next time you need to refer to it. Remember to keep documents that pertain to ongoing questions or updates in either your blue "Waiting for Response" or red "Action Needed" file until you have completed all the required tasks associated with them. Then, move them into your Organizational files for safekeeping and future reference.

Knowing that you have a system and that you are organized will help the whole project seem much more manageable.

Document Discovery and Status Checklist

As you locate and put each document in its designated folder or file, mark off the appropriate box in the checklist below to indicate its status:

- **"Completed"** – all actions are completed.
- **"In the Works"** – you are contacting others for the document or the work is incomplete.
- **"Future"** – you have not yet taken action on this item.

Don't fret about the items that you check off as "Future." Remember, this is a very complex and detailed process. Eventually, you'll cover all the topics. It just takes time. Keep this and all your other worksheets in your binder.

To download the worksheets online, please visit my site, http://susanalpertconsulting.com/downloads/.

Assessment Worksheet:
Government and Civil Documents

1. Government and Civil Documents	Completed	In the Works	Future
Social Security card (If not available, get the number.)			
Passport or citizenship papers			
Driver's license (If not available, get the number, issuing state, and expiration date.)			
Marriage certificate			
Divorce and separation agreements (where relevant)			
Adoption papers			
Military discharge papers			
Death certificate (Order a minimum of 15 copies.)			
Agreement for postal box—U.S. Postal Service and independent service providers			
Utilities statements (Transfer accounts if applicable.)			

2. Legal Documents	Completed	In the Works	Future
Current will			
Trusts—family, charitable, estate			
Power of attorney			
Health care directive			
Estate documents—owner-ship, partnership			
Property titles and deeds			
Real estate partnership papers			
Investment documents—domestic (United States) and abroad			
Business ownership or part-nership papers			
Retirement contracts			

3. Financial Documents —Assets	Completed	In the Works	Future
Bank account statements— savings, checking, trust, safe deposit box			
Investment statements— brokerage accounts, stocks, bonds, coins, collections, cash, gold, silver			
Retirement benefit plans— pensions, IRA, 401(k), SEP, Keogh, etc.			
Tax shelters			
Personal and business tax returns for last two years			
Agreement for safe deposit box (Remember to look in all bank vault storage and any personal safes for valu-ables, such as jewelry, and additional documents.)			
Agreements for other "valu-ables storage"—rented storage space, fur storage, boat storage, art on loan to museums, etc.			

3. Financial Documents—Assets, cont'd	Completed	In the Works	Future
Insurance policies—life, long-term care, estate, Veterans Administration, mortgage, etc.			
Appraisals and inventories of valuable items—IRS Form 706 Step-up Basis			
Outstanding loans to individuals and businesses			
Gift certificates and gift cards			
Airline mileage accounts (Transfer mileage to a family member's account.)			

4. Financial Documents — Liabilities	Completed	In the Works	Future
Mortgages/Leases			
Unpaid tax bills			
Credit card statements for accounts in joint names and/or exclusive to your spouse			
Unpaid bills—hospital, funeral, care facility			
Business debt paperwork			
Outstanding loans and payment plans—automobile, education, equipment, etc.			
Personal debt paperwork—monies owed to/from a relative or friend, maybe not in a legal document			

Update Your Professional Team

Now that you have organized and sorted your documents, what do you do with them?

If you have a Professional Team, speak with them. They probably have already requested that you locate some of these papers. Give your team an update.

If you have been working closely with financial and investment managers, it's quite possible that they will have records of your accounts, investments, retirement plans, etc. If you don't have this information readily available, it's essential that you track down and inform the appropriate parties identified in the "Financial Documents" section of the Document Discovery and Status Checklist. They must be notified as soon as possible.

The work in Phase 2 is intensive and extensive. There are a lot of phone calls to make, paperwork to find and organize, and documents to manage. Some of these contact activities are critical, and some – while important – are less time-sensitive. This less-urgent group of contacts and communications comprises your B-List.

The B-List

Your A-List is made up of your immediate contacts: your Professional Team, insurers, and the Social Security Administration. Your B-List is also important, but less urgent, and includes: credit card providers and other creditors.

Credit Cards

Plastic has become a way of life for most of us, but as we all know, this convenience comes at a risk. Whether you're handing your card to a merchant or providing the number and security codes online or over the phone, be mindful that you're taking steps to protect yourself – and your deceased love one – from fraud and identity theft. This transition period is a particularly vulnerable time; you may be distracted, tired, not at your sharpest. Now's the time to take a step back and make sure your credit information is accurate and well managed. (See "Credit Bureaus" below.)

You may have credit cards in your name only, and others you shared with the person you've lost. It's very important that you keep these (as well as copies of the death certificate) at hand and do the following:

- Close joint accounts.
- Cancel cards in the deceased's name.
- If you don't already have one, open at least one account in your name only, or with another selected signer. (This can often be done while closing the joint account.)

Keep only two to four credit cards. You will find that you really don't need more. In today's world, almost every place you go accepts a major credit card. Use the one of your choice, and have the others (or if your comfort zone dictates, more than the suggested number) as backup. This will simplify tracking bills, decrease the number of payments, and reduce the chance of loss or fraud.

Change Name and Primary Contact Information

This is intensive work, so be prepared. Your long hours and sometimes frustrating circumstances will be rewarded. You'll be dealing with large organizations and need to have your account numbers available. Refer to the documentation you identified, organized, and took action on earlier in this phase and to your Document Discovery and Status Checklist. You'll be relieved to see that you've done a lot of this work.

Other Creditors

Check with the major credit bureaus to guarantee that there are no outstanding debts against your name or that of your lost loved one. Generally, it's just a smart and comprehensive precaution; being thorough could reveal unexpected errors or surprises that need to be addressed.

Credit Bureaus
- Equifax: (800) 525-6285, http://equifax.com
- Experian: (888) 397-3742, http://www.experian.com
- TransUnion: (800) 680-7289, http://www.transunion.com

To download the worksheets online, please visit my site, http://susanalpertconsulting.com/downloads/.

B-List Providers Checklist

CREDIT CARDS

Major Credit Cards	Major Credit Card No. 1
Company/Bank Name:	
Card number:	
Cardholder name:	
Telephone:	
Fax:	
E-mail:	

Major Credit Cards	Major Credit Card No. 2
Company/Bank Name:	
Card number:	
Cardholder name:	
Telephone:	
Fax:	
E-mail:	

Major Credit Cards	Major Credit Card No. 3
Company/Bank Name:	
Card number:	
Cardholder name:	
Telephone:	
Fax:	
E-mail:	

Major Credit Cards	Major Credit Card No. 4
Company/Bank Name:	
Card number:	
Cardholder name:	
Telephone:	
Fax:	
E-mail:	

Major Credit Cards	Major Credit Card No. 5
Company/Bank Name:	
Card number:	
Cardholder name:	
Telephone:	
Fax:	
E-mail:	

Major Credit Cards	Major Credit Card No. 6
Company/Bank Name:	
Card number:	
Cardholder name:	
Telephone:	
Fax:	
E-mail:	

Store Credit Cards	Store Credit Card No. 1
Company Name:	
Card number:	
Cardholder name:	
Telephone:	
Fax:	
E-mail:	

Store Credit Cards	Store Credit Card No. 2
Company Name:	
Card number:	
Cardholder name:	
Telephone:	
Fax:	
E-mail:	

Store Credit Cards	Store Credit Card No. 3
Company Name:	
Card number:	
Cardholder name:	
Telephone:	
Fax:	
E-mail:	

Store Credit Cards	Store Credit Card No. 4
Company Name:	
Card number:	
Cardholder name:	
Telephone:	
Fax:	
E-mail:	

Store Credit Cards	Store Credit Card No. 5
Company Name:	
Card number:	
Cardholder name:	
Telephone:	
Fax:	
E-mail:	

Store Credit Cards	Store Credit Card No. 6
Company Name:	
Card number:	
Cardholder name:	
Telephone:	
Fax:	
E-mail:	

PAYMENT PLANS
(merchant installment plans, planned giving programs)

Payment Plan	Payment Plan No. 1
Company/Organization:	
Account number:	
Telephone:	
Fax:	
E-mail:	

Payment Plan	Payment Plan No. 2
Company/Organization:	
Account number:	
Telephone:	
Fax:	
E-mail:	

LOANS

Home Loan	Mortgage No. 1
Lender:	
Account number:	
Telephone:	
Fax:	
E-mail:	

Home Loan	Mortgage No. 2
Lender:	
Account number:	
Telephone:	
Fax:	
E-mail:	

Home Loan	Equity Line of Credit
Lender:	
Account number:	
Telephone:	
Fax:	
E-mail:	

Auto Loan	Auto Loan No. 1
Lender:	
Account number:	
Telephone:	
Fax:	
E-mail:	

Auto Loan	Auto Loan No. 2
Lender:	
Account number:	
Telephone:	
Fax:	
E-mail:	

Other Loan	Other Loan No. 2
Lender:	
Account number:	
Telephone:	
Fax:	
E-mail:	

Other Loan	Other Loan No. 2
Lender:	
Account number:	
Telephone:	
Fax:	
E-mail:	

LEASES

(automobile, equipment, residential property, business property)

Lease	Lease No. 1
Lessor:	
Contact name:	
Telephone:	
Fax:	
E-mail:	

Lease	Lease No. 2
Lessor:	
Contact name:	
Telephone:	
Fax:	
E-mail:	

UNPAID BILLS

(taxes, hospital, healthcare facility, funeral expenses)

Unpaid Bill	Unpaid Bill No. 1
Company:	
Account number:	
Telephone:	
Fax:	
E-mail:	

Unpaid Bill	Unpaid Bill No. 2
Company:	
Account number:	
Telephone:	
Fax:	
E-mail:	

BUSINESS DEBT

Business Debt	Business Debt No. 1
Company:	
Account number:	
Telephone:	
Fax:	
E-mail:	

Business Debt	Business Debt No. 2
Company:	
Account number:	
Telephone:	
Fax:	
E-mail:	

Your New Roadmap

You may be wondering how much more work can possibly be left to do. What else do I have to handle? It has taken so much energy and time to complete the Chaos to Control phases so far, now what?

Actually, you're on the home stretch. If you've worked through Phases 1 and 2, you've gathered and assessed the pieces you'll need to move ahead. You've done good work. Hard work.

Your dedication, time, and energy have paid off: Without this work, you'd still be surrounded by bedlam. You're not. There's now a plan, a path to take, and an order to the process.

Because of your work, many of the tasks you now face have been "inadvertently" completed. Every time you communicated with someone, wrote a note, filed a form, and so on, you were combining actions – even though it was not your primary focus at the time. It just happened.

When you started this process, you had only just begun your journey from Chaos to Control. You were surrounded by paperwork and were faced with a new life. You had no map in hand. No course to take. It was overwhelming.

Now, your new roadmap is drawn. You have documented your journey. And you are prepared to move confidently forward.

It's now time to tackle the niggling details and wrap up the loose ends. Your work will continue – new paperwork will arrive, the phone will continue to ring, and a long-lost "something" will need attention. But you've handled the bulk of it.

In Phase 3, you'll set your future plan in motion by reviewing your documents, evaluating, and planning.

PHASE 3 STEPS

Step A:	**Document Review**
Step B:	**Updates and Cancellations**
Step C:	**Finance Evaluation**
Step D:	**Professional Team Reconnect**

Step A: Document Review

Here's where you make sure everything is in order – that you have all the documents you need and that you know the status of all of your work.

Review, Assess, Complete

Open your folders and files, and take a close look at all of your paperwork. Review the checklists from Phase 2 ("Document Discovery and Status Checklist," "B-List Providers Checklist"), plus the blue "Waiting for Response" and red "Action Needed" files you created in Phase 1.

Address Items Still Pending, Push to Complete

Now's the time to complete, as best you can for now, what is requested of you:

- Have you responded to all immediate and essential requests?
- Which companies do you still need to inform of your loss? What do they require of you?
- Reminder: Have you changed the ownership, title, and mailing name, where appropriate?

Step B: Updates and Cancellations

Next, it's time to cancel or reinstate accounts and items in your name only, if not completed in Phase 2: Assessment. A starting list of these items follows below; everyone's list is personal and different. You will find a more detailed checklist at the end of Phase 3. *[See the worksheet "Updates and Cancellations Checklist" at the end of Phase 3.]*

These tasks had been assigned to the "Future" column on your Document Discovery and Status Checklist, not because they were *unimportant* but because there were *other, higher priorities.*

As you work through these tasks, you will need the following in hand: account numbers, registration IDs, passwords, and in many instances, copies of death certificates.

Cancel or Change Ownership

- Mobile devices (e.g., cell phone, Kindle, iPad)
- Social networks (e.g., Facebook, LinkedIn, Twitter)
- Automobile and other registrations not already transferred or cancelled
- Periodical and other subscriptions
- E-mail accounts
- Utilities (Transfer if appropriate/applicable.)
- Professional and social memberships and listings
- Airline mileage (Transfer miles to your name. If you have membership in the same airline, almost all carriers will assist with this.)
- Mailing lists (Contact individual membership organizations or other groups whose correspondence had been elected to be received; e.g., alumni groups, charitable organizations.)
- Direct mail and telemarketing lists (Reduce unsolicited offers for credit cards and insurance by calling the national

credit reporting agencies' opt-out line at (888) 567-8688; to change your direct mail preferences, contact the Direct Marketing Association at http://www.dmachoice.org or (212) 768-7277; and to get off lists for telemarketing, contact the Do Not Call Registry at http://www.donotcall.gov or (888) 382-1222.)

- Other categories that are unique to your situation and not determined earlier

Research/Investigate

- Unclaimed property – in the state of present domicile and all others
- Property under a different name
- Un-cashed traveler's checks

Miscellaneous

This includes anything else that you question, or even vaguely recall, or that occurs to you at a later date. Don't be surprised if new information "pops into your head" for quite some time – even after you think you have completed all your work.

Response, Not Reaction

The difference in "rediscovering" information – whether it's truly new or just newly remembered – is how you respond to your situation. Since you have been following the Chaos to Control method, surprises will not overwhelm you. You'll know just what to do, will have the resources to find answers or direction, and know whom to call for guidance. You are solid.

To download the worksheets online, please visit my site, http://susanalpertconsulting.com/downloads/.

Updates and Cancellations Checklist

Cancel or Change Ownership

Mobile Devices		
Cell phone		
Electronic reader (e.g., Kindle, Nook)		
Tablet computer (e.g., iPad)		
Other		

Social Networks		
Facebook		
LinkedIn		
Twitter		
Other		

E-mail Accounts		
E-mail Account 1		
E-mail Account 2		

Automobile Title/ Registration	Completed	Note:
Auto 1		
Auto 2		

Other Vehicle Title/Registration		
Boat		
Airplane		
RV		
Motorcycle		
Personal watercraft (e.g., Jet Ski)		
Snowmobile		
Other		

Airline Mileage Accounts	Completed	Note:
Airline 1		
Airline 2		
Airline 3		
Airline 4		

Utilities	Completed	Note:
Telephone (land line only)		
Electricity		
Gas		
Water		
Garbage		
Recycling		
Cable (TV/Internet/digital phone)		
Satellite		
Internet		

Professional Memberships	Completed	Note:
Professional group 1		
Professional group 2		
Professional group 3		

Social Memberships	Completed	Note:
Social Organization 1		
Social Organization 2		
Social Organization 3		
Social Organization 4		

Other Paid Memberships	Completed	Note:
Other Membership 1		
Other Membership 2		
Other Membership 3		
Other Membership 4		

Charitable Organizations	Completed	Note:
Charitable Organization 1		
Charitable Organization 2		
Charitable Organization 3		
Charitable Organization 4		

Periodicals / Subscriptions	Completed	Note:
Subscription 1		
Subscription 2		
Subscription 3		
Subscription 4		

Other Requested Mailing Lists	Completed	Note:
Other Mailing List 1		
Other Mailing List 2		
Other Mailing List 3		

Direct Mail Opt-Out	Completed	Contact:
Direct Marketing Association		http://www.dmachoice.org (212) 768-7277
National credit reporting agencies' opt-out line		(888) 567-8688

Telemarketing Opt-Out	Completed	Contact:
Do Not Call Registry		http://www.donotcall.gov (888) 382-1222

Other	Completed	Note:
Other 1		
Other 2		
Other 3		

Step C: Finance Evaluation

It's very natural – and common – to worry about your long-term financial status when you're suddenly confronted with such a major change in your plans. Now that you've dealt with your overwhelming present, it's time to address these concerns and create a clear plan for the future.

Most people start by imagining the worst-case scenario. *This worst-case scenario often is not true.* But you still can't stop wondering:

- What is the impact of this transition?
- Will I have to change my lifestyle?
- What will I do?
- Where do I start?

Your accountant and financial advisors are the link to your answers to these questions. You may have some of your information at hand but may be missing pieces. Your experts may have information to contribute, too. Together, you'll define a more detailed picture. Here's where you make that happen.

Your Financial Work

- **Assets and liabilities:** You defined your assets and liabilities in earlier work. These listings are a good indication of your present financial picture.

- **Spending:** Determine what you've spent – on a monthly and annual basis. Not too many people keep accurate and detailed records of anything other than major expenditures. The lesser ones add up very quickly.

- **Credit Cards:** Access your annual credit card summaries as a first-round spending guide. (Contact your individual card issuers for annual summaries if you do not have them.) Take into consideration the different cards you use and how much you pay in cash.

- **Budget:** Some individuals and families establish and work within an annual budget. This is a good place to start, as the work you have already done provides you with more information than someone starting from scratch. Once you have gathered and reviewed your spending record, you'll have everything you need to create a new budget based on your current situation and long-term financial goals.

Your Life, Your Finances

On the following pages, you'll find a generic, broad overview of budgeting elements to consider. Your situation is individual and unique, but what's important is to estimate, as best as possible, what it would cost to live the life you were leading before your loss.

Once this is complete, you may find that you do not have to make any changes in your lifestyle. You know your net worth, liabilities, and spending record. On the other hand, you may clearly see that you need to adjust. If this is the case, take a deep breath ... and get ready to make another list.

Create a Generic Budget List

Start at the beginning, by separating the "must have" from the "nice to have" items in your life. As you work through the categories below, fill in the line items that pertain to you in the "**Personal Budget Worksheet**" provided on page 167.

Essentials

These are the very basic expenses – what is needed to keep a roof over your head, the lights on, clothes on your back, and healthy food in your refrigerator:

- Clothing
- Food (groceries only; not dining out)
- Housing (rent or mortgage, including property taxes and insurance if you own your home)
- Utilities (telephone, water, gas, electricity, garbage collection – not cable, satellite, or Internet)
- Furniture and basic appliances
- Transportation (bus, taxi, bicycle, automobile plus gas)
- Health care

Lifestyle vs. Luxury

You will need to ponder the following list to determine what each item represents for you. Which items are truly needed to maintain your basic comforts, and which are "luxuries" that you could manage without?

- Household furnishings and decor
- Personal computer
- Internet access
- Mobile electronic devices (e.g., cell phone, Kindle, iPad)
- Cable or satellite TV
- Household help (e.g., housekeeper, gardener, nanny)
- Dining out
- Entertainment
- Travel
- Gifts
- Hobby supplies
- Pets

- Education (e.g., school, music lessons, extracurricular classes)
- Additional automobiles/trucks
- Recreational vehicles (e.g., boat, snowmobile, RV)
- Jewelry and accessories

Review, Adjust, Review

Carefully review these budget lists and estimate the monetary cost of each item and activity.

This is a fact-finding mission to discover how much you really spend on what and when. Be honest with yourself. Do not judge. Simply identify and record.

Once you have the information in front of you, evaluate it as objectively as possible and consider adjustments.

This is a beginning. Do not make rash assessments, form opinions, or take action at this time. Simply work through the budget categories and detail. You will make changes. This is OK.

Budget Worksheet

Our budgeting worksheet takes a straightforward, streamlined approach, so you can easily repurpose it for your individual needs. You can use the pencil-and-paper version on page 167 or access the online worksheet, which will calculate your subtotals for you. Simply visit: http://susanalpertconsulting.com/downloads/

This example will get you starting to think and plan. There are many more free budgets templates and budgeting tools available online. Your Professional team and financial institutions may also provide or suggest resources. If you choose to enroll in the Chaos to Control program, we can also help you develop a detailed, customized version just for you.

Structure your budget in the format that works best for you.

Step D: Updates and Cancellations

Call in the Experts

If you have a Professional Team, talk to your financial experts. They will shed much light, bring additional expertise, and assist you with decisions. *Take your time.*

Revise Your List

Most of us find that this work is difficult on an emotional as well as financial basis. It's frightening, no matter what the results. Money is a delicate topic, and if you haven't had sole responsibility for meeting the financial needs of your household, it is natural to feel burdened and unsettled. It *does* get resolved and manageable over time.

Now that you're armed with facts, figures, and professional advice, take your original lists and revise them into a workable plan.

Don't worry if you don't live exactly within this first, revised budget. As with many tasks that you're undertaking, you will experience trial and error, and make changes based on what you learn. You've created a guideline, and that's a great accomplishment. With each passing month, you'll make adjustments in this important and encompassing area, as well as in the rest of your life.

Looking Forward

Now it's time to consider additional forward action. Take time to absorb new information, talk to your team, research options, and perhaps get other opinions.

Most importantly, be informed and receptive. Ultimately, the decisions are yours, but you are now in a position to better comprehend the business aspects of your personal life.

Let Strength Propel Your Future

It has taken you a long time to get to this point. You can confidently address the practical aspects of your loss. Your new road in life still presents many unknowns, but what is known and clear is that you've overcome an incredible obstacle and have emerged victorious. The next step – investigating new ideas and viewpoints in order to start making investments and diversifying – will move you even farther down the road of independence. But for now, take a moment to appreciate what you have accomplished.

You have successfully navigated and completed what seemed insurmountable in the beginning. Take time to appreciate how far you've come. Realize how much independence you've gained; how much you have learned; how strong, powerful, and capable you are; and that you are now in the position to help others.

The business of grief is the outcome of personal pain and the resulting awareness that one person can make a difference. You've excelled. Perhaps you can now share your knowledge and insights with others.

Take your personally-defined roadmap and continue to define your new direction, your path ahead. The journey is different, and it is your own.

To download the worksheets online, please visit my site, http://susanalpertconsulting.com/downloads/.

Personal Budget Worksheet

COLUMN A		COLUMN B	
HOUSING	**Projected Cost $**	**ENTERTAINMENT**	**Projected Cost $**
Mortgage or rent		Video/DVD	
Phones: landline, mobile		CD, MP3, other format	
Electricity		Movies	
Gas		Concerts, theater	
Water and sewer		Sporting events	
Cable		Other	
Waste removal		Petty cash	
Furnishings		Travel/vacation	
Supplies		Other	
Maintenance		*Subtotals*	
Repairs			
Design			
Improvements/remodel			
Security			
Other			
Subtotals			

COLUMN A		COLUMN B	
TRANSPORTATION	**Projected Cost $**	**LOANS**	**Projected Cost $**
Vehicle payments		Major credit card 1	
Insurance		Major credit card 2	
Licensing		Major credit card 3	
Fuel		Store credit card 1	
Maintenance fund		Store credit card 2	
Other		Store credit card 3	
Subtotals		Payment plans –Org. 1	
		Payment plans –Org. 2	
FOOD	**Projected Cost $**	Autos	
Groceries		Leases (equipment, property)	
Dining out		Unpaid bills (taxes, hospital, etc.)	
Club/lounge		Business debt 1	
Coffee		Business debt 2	
Other		Other	
Subtotals		*Subtotals*	

COLUMN A		COLUMN B	
INSURANCE	**Projected Cost $**	**SAVINGS OR INVESTMENTS**	**Projected Cost $**
Health		Retirement accounts – IRA, 401K	
Life		Investment accounts – direct	
Long-term care		Other investment 1	
Casualty		Other investment 2	
Personal		Other investment 3	
Personal umbrella		Other investment 4	
Property (rental/ homeowner)		Other investment 5	
Mortgage		*Subtotals*	
Business			
Valuables		**DONATIONS & MAJOR GIFTS**	**Projected Cost $**
Autos		Charity 1	
Other vehicles (boat, RV, etc.)		Charity 2	
Travel		Charity 3	
Other		Charity 4	
Subtotals		Charity 5	
		Other	
		Subtotals	

COLUMN A		COLUMN B	
MEDICAL – OUT OF POCKET	**Projected Cost $**	**GIFTS**	**Projected Cost $**
Physicians		Annual gifts (birthday, anniversary)	
Alternative		Discretionary (grandchildren, etc.)	
Pharmacy		Holiday	
Other		Other	
Grooming		*Subtotals*	
Toys			
Other		**PERSONAL CARE**	**Projected Cost $**
Subtotals		Clothing	
		Hair	
		Grooming services	
		Grooming & cosmetic products	
		Fitness	
		Dry cleaning, laundry	
		Organization dues & fees	
		Other	
		Subtotals	

COLUMN A		COLUMN B	
TAXES	**Projected Cost $**	**LEGAL**	**Projected Cost $**
Federal		Attorney	
State		Accountant	
Local		Administrator	
Property		Life Lock, Identity Guard	
Other		Other	
Subtotals		*Subtotals*	

COLUMN A: Projected Cost	COLUMN B: Projected Cost

Total Projected Cost (Col A & B):	

PROJECTED MONTHLY INCOME	**$**
Income source 1	
Income source 2	
Income source 3	
Income source 4	
Subtotals	

I may not have gone where I intended to go,
but I think I've ended up where I needed to be.
~Douglas Adams~

Larry and Sue Alpert

ACKNOWLEDGMENTS

To my daughters, Dana and Bari, their husbands, Steve and Sean, and my beautiful grandchildren, Jason, Alexa, Matthew, Cade, Hope, and Shane: I would never have made it through the last few years without your strength, and unconditional love. You are my treasure, and your mere existence has been my greatest source of joy and pride.

To all of my dear friends who held me up through the most tragic period of my life: Many of you flew across the country or drove in from other parts of the state to make sure I knew that I was not alone. From groceries, to hugs, to offering a shoulder to cry on, you went out of your way to bring me back from the depths of my despair, and I will never forget one moment of the salvation you gave to me. It would take another book to properly thank, or even list, you all by name. But you know who you are. The aura of your love still shines brightly for me. Thank you from the bottom of my heart for being in my life.

To my grief therapist, Marilyn Kaplan, and my team of professional advisors, Barry Porter, Gary Kramer, and John Stillman: You have my undying gratitude for all your help in getting my life back in order after Larry died. Without your support, and everything you taught me, I would not have been able to write this book.

To the team of editors and graphic artists, Taylor Mallory Holland, Judy Lewenthal Daniel, Michael Levin, Laura Fredrickson Daly, and Maria McLaughlin: Thank you all so much for the hard work and dedication to this project. Your talent and creativity helped me give life to my dream of helping others navigate the overwhelming business of grief, and for that, I am most grateful.

Made in the USA
San Bernardino, CA
24 November 2014